ALICE BRADBURY
AND SHARON VINCE

FOOD BANKS IN SCHOOLS AND NURSERIES

The Education Sector's Responses to the Cost-of-Living Crisis

First published in Great Britain in 2025 by

Policy Press, an imprint of
Bristol University Press
University of Bristol
1–9 Old Park Hill
Bristol
BS2 8BB
UK
t: +44 (0)117 374 6645
e: bup-info@bristol.ac.uk

Details of international sales and distribution partners are available at
policy.bristoluniversitypress.co.uk

© Bradbury 2025, © Vince 2025

The digital PDF and ePub versions of this title are available open access and distributed under the terms of the Creative Commons Attribution-NonCommercial-NoDerivatives 4.0 International licence (https://creativecommons.org/licenses/by-nc-nd/4.0/) which permits reproduction and distribution for non-commercial use without further permission provided the original work is attributed.

British Library Cataloguing in Publication Data
A catalogue record for this book is available from the British Library

ISBN 978-1-4473-7552-4 paperback
ISBN 978-1-4473-7553-1 ePub
ISBN 978-1-4473-7554-8 OA PDF

The rights of Alice Bradbury and Sharon Vince to be identified as authors of this work have been asserted by them in accordance with the Copyright, Designs and Patents Act 1988.

All rights reserved: no part of this publication may be reproduced, stored in a retrieval system, or transmitted in any form or by any means, electronic, mechanical, photocopying, recording, or otherwise without the prior permission of Bristol University Press.

Every reasonable effort has been made to obtain permission to reproduce copyrighted material. If, however, anyone knows of an oversight, please contact the publisher.

The statements and opinions contained within this publication are solely those of the authors and not of the University of Bristol or Bristol University Press. The University of Bristol and Bristol University Press disclaim responsibility for any injury to persons or property resulting from any material published in this publication.

Bristol University Press and Policy Press work to counter discrimination on grounds of gender, race, disability, age and sexuality.

Cover design: David Worth
Front cover image: Alamy/Lucy Piper
Bristol University Press and Policy Press use environmentally responsible print partners.
Printed and bound in Great Britain by CPI Group (UK) Ltd, Croydon, CR0 4YY

AB: For Alistair
SV: For Mum

Contents

Acknowledgements		vi
one	Why research food banks in schools and nurseries?	1
two	How have the cost-of-living crisis, Covid and austerity affected families and schools?	22
three	How do food banks in schools work, and how did they start?	40
four	What is the impact of food banks on children and their families?	70
five	Why do schools have food banks?	100
six	Where is policy? Schools, responsibility and the withdrawal of the state	128
Notes on anti-poverty and food campaigners		152
References		154
Index		168

Acknowledgements

We wish to acknowledge first of all our research participants who gave their time to talk to us about their schools and nurseries, their food banks and their local community. We were warmly welcomed into many settings and schools, shown the food bank in operation or the rooms where it is organised, and many people made an effort to ensure we were able to find out as much as possible.

We are also immensely grateful to the British Education Research Association for funding the Food Banks in Schools project, and the Monday Charitable Trust for funding the Food Banks in Early Years Settings project. We are also grateful for the support of the Helen Hamlyn Trust, whose funding of the Helen Hamlyn Centre for Pedagogy enabled Alice to spend time on these projects. We also want to thank HHCP Centre Manager Monika Ozdzynska for her help in organising the fieldwork and Becky Trollope for helping with some interviews. We are also grateful to the wider HHCP team for helping to organise seminars on this work, especially Ghassan Essalehi.

We are indebted to our colleagues with whom we have discussed this work, particularly Will Baker at Bristol University, who shared useful information with us from the start, and Gurpinder Lalli at Wolverhampton, who has long been interested in schools and food. We look forward to reading Will's emerging work on this area and further engagement with both. Thank you to Carol Vincent for her advice on home–school relationships, Bronwen Jones for reading our argument on responsibility, and Gemma Moss for the useful discussions on Covid and continued crises of poverty. This project emerged from work Alice conducted with Gemma during the pandemic which found food was a major issue for many schools in providing for families during lockdowns, and Gemma has been supportive of these projects and their focus on schools within their communities.

On a more personal note, Alice wishes to thank her family for understanding when I had to spend weekends writing this book, and particularly my husband Alistair for his support. The book is dedicated to him, for my part. As ever, I am grateful to my mum for helping with the children and giving me some space to think, and to my friends and wider family for their encouragement. These projects have been motivated entirely by a desire to bring the problem of child poverty to wider prominence, and I hope that we have been able, along with many other researchers and organisations, to do so.

Sharon is grateful to her husband, Alex, for his patience and understanding, especially on those nights when writing went on late into the night. Thanks go, too, to friends, family, colleagues and students for their support and encouragement. Finally, thanks to Alice for providing the opportunity to work on such an important project.

ONE

Why research food banks in schools and nurseries?

Introduction

This book is about how growing levels of child poverty have resulted in schools and early years settings stepping beyond their educational purpose to feed hungry families during the cost-of-living crisis. Schools, nurseries, nursery schools and pre-schools (hereafter termed schools) offer free food to families in need, through food banks which operate on-site, in various forms. There are, in fact, more food banks *in schools* in England than in wider society, according to 2024 figures (Baker et al, 2024). Research suggests over 80 per cent of schools offer some form of free food to families, well beyond the usual free lunches and breakfast clubs traditionally provided (Lucas et al, 2023).

Our focus is on food for families, but also on the other provision that goes alongside this: free or heavily subsidised clothing, shoes, toiletries and baby equipment, for example. While the value of providing free food to children through free school meals (FSM) and breakfast clubs is generally accepted (Bogiatzis-Gibbons et al, 2021; Cohen et al, 2021), there is far less research on what schools provide for the wider family, and the effects, or on the impact of non-food goods. Building on

Will Baker and colleagues' groundbreaking research on food charity in schools (Baker & Bakopoulou, 2022; Baker, 2023; Baker et al, 2024), we aim here to shed further light on the way in which food banks in schools operate, the impact on children, families and staff, and the reasons why schools feel they need to offer a food bank. Drawing on case studies of 12 primary schools and early years settings, we explore through interview data how the education sector has come to be so significant in alleviating child poverty, and the combination of moral and practical motivations for organising food banks. We consider why families find food banks in schools less stigmatising, how the food bank phenomenon relates to discourses of reducing 'food waste', and why schools are effective sites for food banks aimed at families.

This book is not about *how or why* child poverty came to be so high – that issue is explored in depth in wider literature (Ridge, 2013; Treanor, 2020) – we focus on the issue of *responsibility*, and the responsibilisation of schools to address children's hunger and wider needs. We are interested in what this means in terms of education policy, particularly the implications of the state relying on schools to address families' welfare needs while failing to fund or recognise this work. The policy vacuum around child poverty and schools has been filled by well-meaning, hard-working and caring education staff, who, when faced with hungry children and parents, have chosen to step in. That is not, we argue, a sustainable solution to the problem of child poverty; in the high-stakes accountability-driven education sector, it leaves widely uneven burdens on some schools in some areas. This work either needs to be recognised and funded, or an equally effective solution found.

While our focus in on education, we build on the extensive literature on public food banks as evidence of the retrenchment of the welfare state, within a neoliberal ideology that individualises responsibility. Many researchers have argued that the establishment of food banks as a 'normal' response to food insecurity symbolises the delegation of responsibility for a fundamental right to food to charities and civic organisations (Riches, 2002; Lambie-Mumford, 2017). We argue that food banks in schools are similarly a response to the reduction of state support, where another state-funded organisation steps in to solve the problem of children's hunger. The ideology of individualisation which underpins the reduction in support for those in need cannot take into account the moral and ethical responses of the school staff, who see caring for children as part of their professional identity. There is a tension between the 'stepping away' of one part of the state, and the 'stepping in' of schools, inherent in the movement of educational institutions beyond their purely educational purposes. This we see as problematic, because school food banks, like public food banks, resolve the problem without addressing the cause; they are a mere sticking plaster. However, we also see food banks in schools as a sign of hope and care, where human interaction and recognition of need supersedes any formal structure of responsibility.

This first chapter sets out our rationale for the research, which relates to the cost-of-living crisis in the early 2020s, and some background on the primary and early years education sectors. We then set out the theoretical framework for our analysis, and set out our research design and methods. A final part of the chapter sets out the structure of the remaining chapters.

Rationale for the research: the cost-of-living crisis

We come to this book as two sociologists of education, focused on primary and early years education policy, with experience ourselves as teachers and as parents. We began thinking together about food banks in schools in June 2021, as we emerged from the Covid crisis. Alice had been researching primary education responses to Covid with Institute of Education (IOE) colleagues (Moss et al, 2020; Bradbury et al, 2022; Moss et al, 2021), and one factor had stood out from this work – the importance of food. Headteachers' first concerns when schools shut were children's safety and then children's hunger. Concerns about 'learning loss' were the preserve of those in more affluent areas. Schools became the main point of contact with the state for many families in the Covid era, providing advice and a sense of community when everything else fell away. Conversations with Sharon about how this was working in the early years settings she was researching led us to begin a project looking at schools operating food banks (funded by British Education Research Association (BERA)) (Bradbury & Vince, 2023), and then a sister project looking at early years settings (funded by the Monday Charitable Trust) (Bradbury & Vince, 2024).

As we began fieldwork, the public consciousness of food banks in schools grew, as the cost-of-living crisis began to unfold. This followed growing awareness of food banks in general during the 2010s due to austerity policies. The cost-of-living crisis is defined by high inflation, increases in energy prices, stagnant wages and lower living standards, and was particularly acute during the winter of 2022–23, when we were conducting fieldwork in schools, where there were significant concerns about families choosing between 'heating or eating'. There was also widespread concern about the health and social impacts of the crisis (Patrick & Pybus, 2022). Press reports covered the impact in schools, such as a Schools Week article titled 'Schools now "part of the welfare state" as cost of living crisis deepens' (Belger, 2022), which reported on children without electricity at home and wearing too-small and dirty clothes. Research which was published during the course of the projects further emphasised the impact of the cost-of-living crisis on schools, including the finding that 79 per cent of schools in the most deprived quartile were providing food for pupils and their families (Lucas et al, 2023).

As we undertook this research, our views and interests in relation to this topic changed: we realised how the term 'food bank' did not capture the extent of what schools were offering (though it remains a useful short-hand), and we learnt a great deal about the world of food charity. We realised from the start that there was no way to 'measure' the impact of food banks within our research design, but nonetheless we were surprised by the extent of the impact described by staff. We remained, however, interested in *why* schools operate food banks in increasing numbers and what this means for the education sector as a whole. Ultimately, the rationale for this work is, and has always been, that we want people to know what schools are doing for hungry families, so that this work can be properly recognised and funded.

The education context

The operation of food banks in schools cannot be understood without placing this work in the specific context of education in the post-pandemic era of the early 2020s. The period between the Covid crisis and the Labour victory in the General Election of 2024 marked a particular context, politically and socially. After the final Covid restrictions were lifted, further crises followed immediately, with the invasion of Ukraine and rising energy prices and inflation affecting families' finances. Schools had been hugely affected by the Covid crisis, remaining open for the children of key workers and vulnerable children throughout, and having also to organise home learning for the majority of pupils. Early years settings had been closed during the first lockdown but not the second. However much optimism there had been for long-term change in education as a result of the lessons from Covid – including Alice's own 'post-pandemic hopes' (Bradbury, 2021) – the education system very quickly returned to normal. Statutory assessments returned, and the focus turned to redressing lost learning through tutoring, to ensure every child would 'catch up'.

Tensions remained, however, between the increasing pressures faced by schools, particularly on budgets, and the re-establishment of the system of accountability through testing and inspection by Ofsted. After a long decade of

Conservative-led governments' reforms in education, there were a number of problems facing both the primary and early years sectors.

Primary schools from 2010 to the early 2020s

Primary education in this era was dominated by significant policy reform which made major changes to the curriculum and assessment frameworks for children aged 5–11 (the Early Years Foundation Stage is dealt with in the following section although the Reception Year and Nursery classes are both part of primary schools and part of the EYFS). Conservative-led governments in the 2010s introduced a new National Curriculum in 2014, and removed the old system of National Curriculum levels which had been used for assessment. Another major change was the growth of statutory assessment: new assessments were introduced into Year 1 (age 5/6) – the Phonics Screening Check; and into Year 4 with the Multiplication Tables Check. Key Stage 1 SATs tests, taken in Year 2, were continued until 2021, and then made non-statutory. The main assessments of schools at Key Stage 2, Year 6 SATs, continued to form the major method of assessing the quality of a school. These tests, which have been found to be a cause of stress for teachers and children (Wyse et al, 2022; Quick, 2024a), provide the data used in league tables of schools and by Ofsted.

Ofsted remained a major consideration for primary schools during this era, as headteachers responded to changing priorities from the inspectorate. This included a focus on attainment data in the early and mid-2010s, engendering a process of datafication (Bradbury & Roberts-Holmes, 2016), followed by a shift towards the curriculum after the inspection framework changed in 2019 (Perryman et al, 2023). There were also structural changes in the 2010s, including the move to allow primary schools to become academies. By 2020, 35 per cent of primaries were academies, with the vast majority part of multi-academy trusts (MATs); by 2024, the proportion was 43 per cent (UK Government, 2024). Within our sample of schools, we have mainly local authority schools (Booth, Webb, Twining, Lansbury and Rowntree Primary Schools – all pseudonyms) and one academy (Peabody Primary School).

Funding remained a major issue for schools; an Institute for Fiscal Studies analysis found funding levels in real terms would be below 2009 levels, per pupil, in 2023 (IFS, 2021). The National Association of Headteachers raised concerns about the significant cuts needed to manage the shortfall, including reducing the number of teaching assistants and teachers (NAHT, 2022). At the same time, there were serious concerns about teacher retention and recruitment (Perryman, 2022). Thus, at the time of this research, primary schools were under pressure from various sources, as well as managing the impact of both Covid and then the cost-of-living crisis.

The early years sector

While we refer to all of the educational institutions discussed here as 'schools' for ease of reading, we wish to emphasise the important difference between the early years settings and the primary schools here. While maintained nursery schools like our case study settings Field and Rashford Nursery Schools (both pseudonyms) are state-funded schools which cater for younger children, they are part of a complex assemblage of early years provision in England which is dominated by marketisation and the operation of for-profit providers. This context is important in understanding where our sample of settings fits into the overall picture.

The early years sector is a mixed market of private, voluntary and independent (PVI) providers, state-run nursery schools and nursery classes in primary schools, and childminders who look after children in their own homes. Reception classes in primary schools are also part of the statutory Early Years Foundation Stage (EYFS), which has its own curriculum and assessment framework. There are also children's centres, which offer 'stay and play' groups as well as advice and guidance, and sometimes also include a nursery or pre-school. There are distinctions between these different types of setting, which are relevant here.

Maintained nursery schools are few in number and decreasing due to policy decisions, but have an outsized significance in terms of addressing disadvantage among families with younger children (Early Education, 2015). Historically, nursery schools were set up in poorer areas with the aim of educating and caring for children from less affluent backgrounds, allowing parents to work and also attempting to provide children with new opportunities and adequate nutrition (Palmer, 2011). Nursery schools have continued to provide additional support to families, being described as 'on the frontline' of attempts to address poverty (Hoskins et al, 2021). In terms of structure, nursery schools are similar to primary schools in that they have a headteacher who has financial and operational control, and they are funded by the local authority.

PVI nurseries and pre-schools form the majority of the early years sector (Department for Education, 2024). These are not state funded, but do receive funding via parents' entitlement to 15 or 30 hours of childcare (Vince, 2024). PVI settings do not have to employ qualified teachers. In our sample, one pre-school (Brown Pre-School) is a private setting. This sector includes nurseries run by social enterprise organisations, which may cross-subsidise between their nurseries in more affluent areas and those in more disadvantaged areas; two settings in our sample are in this category (Dimbleby and Wilson nurseries).

Children's centres, which emerged from the Sure Start programme of the 2000s, 'provide a wide range of services aimed at supporting parents with young children; these include play groups, parenting support groups, advice on housing, and how to access financial and social support services' (Baker & Bakopoulou, 2022, p 112). Parents usually access children's centres on an ad hoc basis, such as to attend NHS-run sessions, or regularly, such as weekly 'stay and play' sessions, but not every day like in nurseries. Children's centres are staffed by a variety of early years professionals with other specialists attending regularly. We include one children's centre (Oliver Children's Centre) in our sample.

While our analysis in the following chapters includes the data from both the primary schools and early years settings, we sometimes focus on one sector or the other. This allows us to focus in more detail on the distinctiveness of the primary or early years sector and its role in alleviating child poverty. We include these nuances with an awareness that early years is too often the 'forgotten relation' in educational scholarship, and while we use the word 'schools', we wish to emphasise the equal status of the early years within this research.

Theoretical tools

Our theoretical framework for understanding food banks in schools draws on policy sociology, and ideas from the wider sociological literature on responsibilisation, welfare and the state, some of which explores issues of food insecurity more widely. This work has involved us moving beyond our traditional home turf of the sociology of education, into scholarship from social policy, political economy and social geography. Insights from these have proved highly useful in thinking about the bigger picture of education and child poverty, and we explain some of these ideas here before we provide a fuller explanation of the food banks literature in the next chapter.

Policy sociology and enactment

A starting point theoretically has been ideas from policy sociology, even though we are not researching a specific policy. Policy sociology research has often explored what happens in schools and why, considering the inter-relation of political ideas particularly from neoliberalism and the practices present in schools (Ball, 2021). This work is often based on ideas from Michel Foucault, focusing on discourses as dominant sets of ideas and ways of thinking, and how power is enacted (Ball, 2013). We are influenced here by this body of work, including the conceptualisation of how schools 'do policy' as *enactment*, which is affected by the situated, material, professional and external contexts of a school (Braun et al, 2012). However, as we discuss in Chapter Six, the operation of food banks is not a response to policy, but a response *in the absence of a policy* on how schools should manage child hunger. It is more akin to responses to the Covid pandemic described as 'crisis policy enactment' (Bradbury et al, 2022) in the focus on families' immediate needs. This period saw guidance issued to schools at an incredible rate; within three months of the first lockdown being announced in England, the Department for Education had released 50 guidance documents (Fotheringham et al, 2022), leaving education leaders to grapple with what the new recommendations meant for their school (Bradbury et al, 2022). Because guidance was often confusing or contradictory, Bradbury et al found that many education leaders implemented their own policy around the provision of food ahead of official announcements from government. This was driven by the morals and ethics of those working in education and demonstrates how practitioners were willing to act autonomously based upon their in-depth knowledge of the needs of their community. This concept remains useful beyond the Covid period, we argue, in conceptualising the moral and ethical dimensions of why schools run food banks.

We are also influenced by sociological work which considers the subjectivities of those involved in a neoliberal education system, including that which explores how school leaders have been made responsible for schools' outcomes (Keddie, 2015), and work which considers how students have become individually responsibilised (Keddie, 2016; Redmond et al, 2022). This leads into the wider field of responsibility and power.

Power and responsibilisation

The concept of *responsibilisation* is key to our discussions in this book. The term has been used to explain how teachers have been made to feel responsible for the results of children in their school (Keddie, 2015; Done & Murphy, 2018) and for their own self-improvement, within neoliberal discourses of individual responsibility. These link to broader individualising discourses under neoliberalism, which place the onus of responsibility on the individual to make good choices, be a good consumer, recognise their flaws and improve (Bradbury, 2019; Redmond et al, 2022). However, it has rarely been used in educational research to consider the responsibilisation *of the school*, or the education sector as a whole, in this case for their community's welfare needs; this is one of the contributions we wish to make to the literature in this area.

Within social policy scholarship and particularly discussions of food banks in general, the concept of responsibilisation is used slightly differently to mean a context where the state has removed itself from a position of responsibility for hungry families, and instead allowed charities and civic society to take on this responsibility (Riches, 2002; Loopstra & Tarasuk, 2012). Drawing on the examples of the US and Canada where food banks have long been established, scholars argue that the growth of food banks reflects the 'breakdown of the social safety net and the commodification of social assistance' (Riches, 2002, p 648). This wider discussion within the international literature on food banks (or food charity/aid) about the location of responsibility for addressing food poverty is highly relevant to us here. While this argument is established in the literature on food charity, it is rarely extended to food banks in schools, and we wish to make these connections through our analysis.

Researchers have argued that governments across the world, beginning with the US and Canada, but also increasingly in Europe, have allowed third-sector organisations and civil society to solve the problem of hunger, which is caused by government decisions on welfare benefits and the economy (Riches, 2002; Loopstra & Tarasuk, 2012). This shifts the responsibility for addressing hunger (and wider poverty) to these organisations and away from the state, discursively constructing the problem as solved, without ever allowing the root cause of the problem to come into view. In Canada, '[h]unger was being socially constructed as a matter for charity and not the primary obligation of the state' (Riches, 2020, p xii). Politicians visit food banks to praise the volunteers, as Riches (2020) argues, without ever mentioning that there is only a need for the food banks because of their own policies. Thus, as Pickett comments, neoliberalism has driven austerity and the rise of food aid, but also shaped the nature of the provision and 'the way we look at it' (Pickett in Foreword to Power, 2022, pp vii–viii).

We need to consider this political point when exploring food banks in schools. It would be easy to simply see these as a 'good thing', a kind response to children and families in need, and there is no doubt that they are doing some good. But, it is important to note that the argument that the state is absolved of responsibility for hungry children by civil society stepping into the breach is just as relevant to the education sector. As we will see in the following chapters, the complexities of this responsibilisation make this a significant step for schools, who are judged on very different measures from food bank charities. While food banks in schools may not yet represent an 'emergent parallel charity economy' (Riches, 2020, p xii), the questions this body of scholarship asks relating to responsibility are highly relevant to schools.

In this book, we draw on these concepts of enactment, context and responsibilisation to consider schools as a whole, and indeed the education sector as a whole, becoming responsible for the problem of child hunger. Schools have not been instructed to start food banks by government, but staff feel responsible because they are on the frontline, dealing every day with children, face to face. Thus, responsibilisation in this case is complex, with parallels in the wider food bank context, but also areas of distinction. Schools' decisions to act are a key concern for us here, as we explore the significance of food banks for the wider education sector. We turn now to an explanation of how we researched food banks in schools and nurseries.

The research studies

The two studies on which this book is based were conducted in 2022–24. The Food Banks in Schools project was funded by the British Education Research Association, and the Food Banks in Early Years Settings project was funded by the Monday Charitable Trust. Both were also supported by Alice's time allocated to the Helen Hamlyn Centre for Pedagogy at UCL, funded by the Helen Hamlyn Trust. The research team was made up of Alice and Sharon, with one visit conducted by our colleague Becky Trollope due to the time the school requested.

Case study schools and early years settings

For these exploratory qualitative research projects, we took a case study approach, with the aim of building rich case studies of six primary schools in England which had a food bank, or provided free food for families in some way, and six early years settings. The case study schools are conceptualised as 'telling cases' (Mitchell, 1984) which illustrate the pertinent issues, rather than as a representative sample. Our aim in terms of sample was to include variation by region, and variation in terms of local levels of deprivation, bearing in mind the likelihood that schools would be in areas with some deprivation. The sample of six primary schools and six early years settings were accessed through the research team's network of contacts, and through social media via a call for participants. The following tables provide some basic information on the six primary schools (Table 1.1) and early

Table 1.1: Case study schools in the Food Banks in Primary Schools project

Primary school	Description
Booth	Large community primary in a deprived, multi-ethnic area of East London
Lansbury	Community primary in a deprived area of a Midlands city
Peabody	Community primary on the outskirts of London
Rowntree	Small Church of England primary in a deprived town in the North of England
Twining	Small community primary in a deprived, multi-ethnic area of North London
Webb	Community primary in a very mixed area in North London

years settings (Table 1.2). The choice to focus only on primary schools and early years was based on previous research with primary schools providing food during the Covid crisis, and the team's expertise. Our view was that these schools provided examples of how operating a food bank could work, and how it could affect children's learning.

Each school has been allocated a pseudonym to ensure anonymity; these are based on the surnames of anti-poverty campaigners, with the schools' names as historical figures and the early years settings as contemporary figures. Notes on these names are included at the end of the book.

We were successful in including some variation in terms of region, though the case study schools are disproportionately located in London, due to the team's location and networks. The research sites are all located in areas of disadvantage, though to varying extents, and are of different sizes. The locality of the schools also varied, as some were in built-up urban areas, while others were more suburban. In the early years sample, we aimed to include a balance of different types of early years settings given the diverse and fragmented nature of the sector,

Table 1.2: Case study settings in the Food Banks in Early Years Settings project

Early years setting	Description
Brown Pre-School	Pre-school in a village in the North of England
Dimbleby Nursery	Nursery and pre-school run by a social enterprise in Inner London
Field Nursery School	Maintained nursery school in Inner London
Oliver Children's Centre	Children's Centre in Inner London
Rashford Nursery School	Maintained nursery school in a city in the Midlands
Wilson Nursery	Nursery run by a social enterprise in South London

and the final sample included different types of setting: two maintained nursery schools; one private pre-school; two nurseries run by a social enterprise; and one children's centre. In each of these there was free food provided to families at the setting, though the case of the children's centre differed slightly in that a separate organisation used the centre to run a food pantry every week.

Interviews

At each school, our intention was to interview the headteacher or manager, some class teachers and any staff involved in the food bank. In some schools, we were able to also talk to relevant other staff, such as the school cook, and partners from the relevant food provider or charity. In others, we only spoke to senior leaders, although in these cases the leaders were able to give a very detailed account of the school and how the food bank operated. In all cases, we were able to interview someone in a leadership position, except at Oliver Children's Centre where the children's centre staff were not available, and we were limited to speaking to those who run

Table 1.3: List of participants in the Food Banks in Primary Schools project

School	Pseudonym	Role
Booth	Michael	Headteacher
	Matt	Manager of food pantry
	Michelle	Chef
	Mark	Head chef
	Marianne	School support staff involved in food provision
	Martha	Year 6 teacher
Lansbury	Abigail	Headteacher
Peabody	Lorraine	Headteacher
	Lesley	Deputy Headteacher
Rowntree	Charlotte	Headteacher
	Catherine	Year 6 teacher
Twining	Sasha	Headteacher
	Sophie	Year 2 teacher
	Sarah	Support staff leading food bank
Webb	Grace	Headteacher
	Genevieve	Assistant Headteacher

the food pantry, who come from an external organisation. One unanticipated challenge was the disruption caused by industrial action during the spring term of 2023, which meant that we were not able to speak to class teachers in some cases, as they were on strike. Full lists of participants and their roles are provided in Tables 1.3 and 1.4, where all individual names are pseudonyms.

For ethical and practical reasons, we did not interview parents who use the food bank, or their children. While we recognise these voices would have added further detail to the case studies, we made a decision when proposing this research that we did not wish to further burden or stigmatise parents

Table 1.4: List of participants in the Food Banks in Early Years Settings project

Setting	Pseudonym	Role
Brown Pre-School	Helen	Manager
Dimbleby Nursery	Bethany	Manager
	Brenda	Practitioner
	Naomi	Headteacher
	Natalie	Early years practitioner (3- and 4-year-olds' room)
	Nicola	Early years practitioner (2- and 3-year-olds' room)
Field Nursery School	Abigail	Headteacher
	Audrey	Admin officer
	Amelia	Cook
Oliver Children's Centre	Stephanie	Food pantry manager
	Stella	Food pantry volunteer
Wilson Nursery	Gita	Nursery manager
	Gabrielle	Nursery practitioner
	Greg	Chef

who use the food bank and their children by interviewing them. We were also aware that they might be a hard-to-reach population (Wainwright et al, 2024) and we were restricted by time limitations. Gathering data from parents and children is certainly an area for future research, if it can be conducted in sensitive and ethical ways.

The semi-structured interviews for headteachers and managers focused on the perceived impact of the food bank on children, the barriers and challenges involved (including staffing, budgets and equipment), and the overall impact on the school. Teacher and practitioner interviews focused on the impact on children, and particularly on their learning, physical activity and wellbeing. Interviews with other staff were adapted as appropriate to their role, and explored issues such as the practicalities of the foodbank, how families use it and how the school manages the additional workload. For the staff who held a supporting role working with families directly, we also spoke about relationships between parents and school, reducing stigma and wider networks of support.

Some interviews were short, as staff had to return to other duties, while others lasted over an hour. In all cases, interviews were conducted at the school, in locations chosen by the participant. We considered it important to visit all the schools in person, in order to gather information on the wider surroundings and the geography of the school, given the importance of the physical placement on the food bank. We took extensive notes on each visit, but did not conduct any observations. Overall, we found participants to be very keen to explain their work and its impact on children and their families; several participants thanked us for highlighting this under-recognised aspect of their work.

In addition to the interviews in schools, we decided to also interview a staff member (Felicity) at the Felix Project (a food redistribution organisation) as they emerged as a key component of the structure of food banks in schools in the London area. This interview lasted an hour and focused on how they work with schools, how demand has changed and the key purposes of the organisation.

Analysis of the two datasets

All interviews were audio recorded and professionally transcribed and pseudonymised. We analysed the data from each project separately (with schools first) and then returned to the two datasets for a cross-project analysis.

For each project, we analysed the data thematically, based on ideas drawn from the research questions and the literature review. This included adding new themes such as the importance of space and the use of food in the curriculum, as the analysis progressed. Codes were used from the Schools project for the Early Years project, with extra codes arising from the data; however, most themes cut across the two projects. We undertook a process of coding the data individually first, then met as a team to allow for a range of viewpoints and alternative perspectives. Comparing our analyses helped to highlight the different possible readings of the data (not least as only one of us had visited each site) and to clarify any ambiguities in the data. At the stage of analysis combining both projects, we intentionally documented areas of difference between the two sets of case studies, as well as focusing on areas of commonality between the two projects. Eventual findings were agreed by both authors following in-depth discussion of the datasets in conjunction with the wider empirical and theoretical literature.

Ethical issues

The project was approved by the UCL Institute of Education ethical review system, and adhered to the BERA ethical guidelines (BERA, 2018). All participants gave their informed consent to participation and all names of settings and participants have been changed, and any details have been adjusted to ensure that they cannot be identified. Given the sensitivity of the topic of family food poverty, particular care was taken to ensure total anonymity of families who use the food bank. Participants were specifically asked not to name any children or parents during interviews, and they were able to adhere to this guidance. Data were stored safely using the university network and the project adhered to GDPR regulations.

After the interviews, each school was given £50 and each early years setting was given £100 in the form of a donation to their food bank or associated charity, as a thank you for participation (the difference was due to a higher budget). This gift was only communicated after the interviews, so it was not an incentive for participation. We decided as researchers this was an ethical way to thank the respondents for their time, by contributing to the projects we were researching.

Structure of the book

The following chapter reviews the literature on the relationships between education and poverty, including the impact of the austerity policy and the Covid crisis, and the impact of hunger and family stress on children. We also explore what the literature on public food banks has to offer an analysis of school food banks, exploring issues of stigma and the political economy argument that food banks are an example of state retrenchment.

The three main data analysis chapters (Chapters Three, Four and Five) use the data from the 12 case studies to explore three key questions. First, Chapter Three answers the question of how school food banks work, and why families need them. We explore the common models of operation for food banks in schools, and the relationship with food waste reduction organisations, in some cases. This chapter includes a discussion of the 'origin stories' of each food bank, sometimes during Covid and sometimes before, and considers the impact of the cost-of-living crisis on levels of need.

Chapter Four then considers the impact of food banks on children's learning, and the social impacts on their participation in school life and dignity. We explore the impact on families' wellbeing as a whole, and consider the complexity of our participants' views of parents who use the food bank. At times, we find, parents are framed through deficit discourses.

Chapter Five then goes on to explore the reasons why schools run food banks, from the improved relationships that result, to the practical justification of providing food at a convenient site. We consider here the moral and political explanations for the food banks, and the argument that there is simply no one else to solve the problem. This leads into the first part of Chapter Six, which sets out the arguments made by our participants about whether schools *should* have food banks, and potential alternatives. We end the book with a discussion of the potential for disparities between schools to worsen if schools' welfare work is not recognised or funded. We also return to the idea of responsibilisation and our argument that schools have become responsible for alleviating families' food insecurity, because they are faced with the reality of hungry children, and because they care.

TWO

How have the cost-of-living crisis, Covid and austerity affected families and schools?

Introduction

The education sector has in recent years experienced significant challenges due to rising need from communities, as families have struggled with poverty, including experiencing food insecurity. This chapter outlines this context for our food banks in schools projects by exploring existing research on the relationships between poverty and education, the impact of Covid and austerity, and how hunger affects learning and family stress. We also review the literature on community food banks, and detail the key issues relevant to food banks in schools: the role of stigma, the social role of food and how food banks relate to the withdrawal of the state from responsibility for welfare.

The need to spread the net wide in terms of literature arises from the very limited literature in existence on school food banks in England. Baker and colleagues' groundbreaking work in this area provides the only detailed studies of how food banks operate in schools and early years (Baker & Bakopoulou, 2022; Baker, 2023), and on the extent of food banks in education (Baker et al, 2024). Beyond this work, the existing literature on school food focuses in the main on school meals and breakfast clubs (Earl & Lalli, 2020; Bogiatzis-Gibbons et al, 2021; Cohen et al, 2021). Baker's work, using interviews with staff running food banks in schools and early years settings, and with families, provides key insights into the phenomenon of food charity in education. His analysis of the underlying causes focuses on the cost-of-living crisis and a retreating welfare state in England, in a context where charitable food aid is an increasingly socially acceptable response to poverty. Baker concludes that schools are increasingly having to take responsibility in this political context for making sure children's basic needs are met. We argue in a similar fashion that food banks in schools represent a responsibilisation for welfare needs that requires both funding and recognition if we are to address child poverty. We begin our review of the existing research by focusing on this central issue of poverty and education.

The relationships between poverty and education

Education is often presented as a way of escaping poverty, with a human capital approach suggesting that through investing in education, governments can ensure citizens acquire the skills they need to participate in the workforce and earn adequately (Littler, 2017). At the same time, educational attainment is still heavily impacted by income, and the divide begins in the early years, with children from families living on low incomes leaving Reception classes at the age of 4 or 5 years already 4.6 months behind their peers (EPI, 2024). This gap widens to 10.3 months by the end of primary school and 19.2 at the end of secondary (Francis-Devine et al, 2023; EPI, 2024). The relationships between poverty and educational attainment are complex, but research suggests that poverty is a 'barrier to learning' in multiple ways in schools (Mazzoli Smith & Todd, 2019): children from lower-income families struggle with uniform costs, the price of school trips and with clothes for special non-uniform days. This 'in-school stigmatisation of children living in poverty' (Mazzoli Smith & Todd, 2019, p 360) has an affective dimension, as children suffer due to negative social and emotional effects of poverty. A number of policies have been introduced to attempt to mitigate the impact of poverty upon educational attainment, including free school meals (FSM) and the Pupil Premium, additional payments made to schools and early years settings to support children from low-income families (Gooseman et al, 2020). However, none of these addresses the challenges that children living in poverty face *outside* of school. This book considers what schools are doing to help the whole family during this period of multiple crises.

The role of austerity

While in 2010 there were only 35 food banks run by The Trussell Trust across the UK (Sosenko et al, 2019), suggesting that food insecurity was yet to become embedded, through the next decade the term became commonplace (Wells & Caraher, 2014). Austerity measures were introduced by the Conservative and Liberal Democrat Coalition government when they came into power following the 2010 General Election. Wide-reaching cuts to public spending were launched in response to the 2008 global financial crash. However, as Konzelmann (2019) asserts, austerity is also an active political choice: '[Austerity] has also been used for political and ideological reasons (stated or not), as a means of reducing the size and economic role of the state, particularly with respect to social welfare provision' (p 1). Cuts to public spending amounted to £14.3 billion between 2009–10 and 2012–13 (Merrick, 2017), including cuts to education, police, prisons, welfare spending and local authority budgets (O'Hara, 2015). The need for those living on lower incomes to access more public services and receive welfare payments meant that these cuts were not distributed equally across the population (Berman & Hovland, 2024).

Austerity policies had a greater effect on families with children (Ridge, 2013), with cuts to Sure Start Centres (by two-thirds between 2010 and 2018) (Wise, 2021), and other changes including making the Sure Start Maternity Grant available only for first-born children, scrapping the Health in Pregnancy Grant and a reduction in the Child Care element of the Working Tax Credit. Overall, these cuts to benefits amounted to a loss of £1,735 for families on the lowest incomes before a child's first birthday (Ridge, 2013). Wider benefit reforms and shifts in employment also affected families, with issues around the administration of benefits being a main contributor to families needing to use food banks (Sosenko et al, 2019). One of the most devastating welfare policy changes was the two-child benefit cap, whereby child tax credit or Universal Credit would be paid for a third or any subsequent children born into a family from April 2017. It is believed that the policy results in affected families losing out on approximately £3,200 per year per child (Try, 2024) and is a leading reason behind the statistic that 46 per cent of families with three or more children are living in poverty (CPAG, 2024).

At the same time, schools were subject to funding cuts, with government funding on schools falling in real terms; as a result, more than 2,000 headteachers joined a protest at Parliament calling for greater school funding in 2018, an event that was deemed 'unprecedented', with headteachers a group not previously known for such political action (Busby, 2018). With the 'Building Schools for the Future' programme cut in 2010, many schools were now in a state of serious disrepair, with school budgets unable to absorb the cost of repairs (Busby, 2018).

Early years settings saw a similar picture emerge of increased need and funding challenges. Maintained nursery school staff found that they increasingly needed to support families with material goods, including food and clothing (Hoskins et al, 2021), but they were also required to help families with navigating the education system, applying for benefits, accessing healthcare, and signposting parents to training and employment services. In short, early years staff were replacing services, such as Sure Start, that had been stripped away due to austerity, at a time when their own funding had been reduced (Hoskins et al, 2021). Schools, too, took on responsibility for supporting families' welfare in the absence of other services (Baker, 2023).

The impact of the Covid pandemic

The Covid pandemic would have been devastating at any time, yet its arrival following ten years of austerity highlighted the retrenchment of public services.

When it was announced that schools would be closed to most children on 18 March 2020, the problem arose as to how some families would manage to feed children who usually received a free lunch at school (Gaunt, 2020; Lalli, 2023). Indeed, 20.8 per cent of families with children reported experiencing food insecurity during the first two weeks of lockdown (Food Foundation, 2024). The issue was addressed through the provision of either a supermarket voucher or food parcel worth £15 per child per week to be sent to the homes of children eligible for free school meals (Lalli, 2023). During the first lockdown, most schools provided the vouchers, but difficulties with the voucher system meant that headteachers found it hard to order them and families would sometimes discover the voucher did not work when shopping at supermarkets (Lalli, 2023). This contributed to 49 per cent of children entitled to free school meals being unable to access the programme for the first month of lockdown (Parnham et al, 2020). There were wider problems in procuring food at supermarkets with shortages of key items due to stockpiling and ruptures in the food supply chain.

Controversy around the provision of vouchers raged when the government announced that they would only be available during term time, prompting footballer Marcus Rashford to spearhead a campaign calling for the government to reconsider. With widespread media support, the campaign resulted in a government U-turn (Lalli, 2023), and beyond this, Rashford succeeded in highlighting the plight of children living in poverty. Subsequent lockdowns saw the provision of food parcels through schools' catering firms, but some families who were issued with them reported inadequate portions. The government was criticised for utilising private catering companies such as Chartwells to provide the food parcels, suggesting a commitment to privatisation at the expense of children living in poverty.

Despite these challenges to food provision through schools, the proportion of families with children experiencing food insecurity had fallen to 9.6 per cent by January 2021, a significant reduction from 20.8 per cent at the beginning of the first lockdown (Food Foundation, 2024). This reduction is largely credited to a £20 a week increase in Universal Credit payments from April 2020 (Timmins, 2021), a shift towards more welfarist social policy in response to the unprecedented crisis of the pandemic. It was estimated that this increase lifted 400,000 children out of poverty for the brief period (18 months) that the policy existed (JRF, 2023), demonstrating the considerable impact a relatively modest rise in income could have on families' living standards. The support provided by schools and early years settings may also have contributed to this drop in food insecurity experienced by families, as evidence suggests a lack of informal support is one of the three main reasons people use food banks (behind inadequate benefit payments and life events such as unemployment and illness) (Bull et al, 2023).

The hardships that some families encountered during the pandemic changed the work that education settings did, shifting their focus to supporting families with money, food and wellbeing. Unable to see most children in settings, staff would spend time calling families at home. Moss et al (2020) found that, for 72 per cent of school staff, the focus of these conversations was on wellbeing and access to food, compared to only 46 per cent who wanted to discuss whether children were completing school work at home. 52 per cent of headteachers were involved in organising food parcels or a food bank. As Moss and colleagues argue (2020; 2021), education staff support the wider wellbeing of children and families attending their settings due to a sense of moral obligation. They also recognise that children are unlikely to learn if they are hungry. Bradbury et al (2022) argued (using data from the same project) that the Covid pandemic altered how education practitioners regarded government policy and responded to it, resulting in 'crisis policy enactment', as discussed in Chapter One. This is highly relevant for our discussion of how food banks in schools were set up.

Current policy challenges: funding and the cost-of-living crisis

The Covid pandemic was followed immediately by the cost-of-living crisis, a period of sharp inflation with particularly notable increases in the price of energy and food due to a range of factors, including Russia's invasion of Ukraine (Harari et al, 2023). These price rises began at the end of 2021, coinciding with the removal of the £20 a week Universal Credit increase. The drop in income for families on low incomes combined with high inflation has contributed to an increase in food insecurity, with a staggering 26 per cent of all families with children reporting that they were skipping meals or going hungry because they could not afford to buy food in September 2022 (Food Foundation, 2024).

Schools are still in the position of needing to support families, while facing increased costs themselves due to rising energy prices; 80 per cent of schools reported needing to reduce spending elsewhere in order to pay increased fuel bills, while half said they were making cuts in the school budget so they could provide greater support to children and families (Lucas et al, 2023). In this context, this book details some of the measures that schools are taking to provide help to families. We now turn to the literature that explains why food is so important for schools.

Research on hunger, family stress and learning

Biosocial perspectives

We want to preface our discussion of the research on food and learning with a comment on the complexities of the use of 'scientific' research in education. Sociologists of education have a 'longstanding mistrust of biology, due largely to the perception that biology naturalizes and fixes differences' (Youdell & Lindley, 2018, p 1). The association of biological understandings of education with 'fixed ability thinking' (Drummond & Yarker, 2013) and determinism makes many scholars wary, while recent uses of neuroscientific ideas in education have only served to confirm fears that simplistic associations of poverty with 'smaller brains', for example, risk reviving eugenicist ideas (Bradbury, 2021). Despite this mistrust, we engage here with the literature on a less contested area of scholarship focused on hunger and learning, in the spirit of engagement with what Youdell and Lindley call the 'biosocial'. This involves recognising the biological and social entanglements of learning: accepting that biology has something to tell us about learning, alongside psychosocial explanations that focus on relationships, feelings, identities and subjectivities. Thus, Youdell and Lindley (2018) argue that forces that affect learning might also include what we eat, how much we sleep and how much physical activity we engage in. The biosocial assemblage includes all of these features, and need not produce deterministic accounts of who learns well and who doesn't, but might instead allow us to question the production of such inequalities. From this perspective, understanding the importance of food in education is a social justice issue, and to ignore the science due to fears associated with previous misuses of science in education would be misguided.

The impact of hunger on learning and participation

Research suggests that food insecurity can hinder the learning and development of children in different ways depending on the age of the child and the duration of reduced food intake (Ke & Ford-Jones, 2015). For children in the early years, especially infants, inadequate nutrition is particularly detrimental as it can impede the rapid brain development seen during this period (United Nations World Food Programme, 2006; Markowitz et al, 2021). Along with the general malaise that can accompany inadequate food intake, lack of nutrients may result in the very young being less likely to play and explore the world around them, which is crucial for their development (United Nations World Food Programme, 2006). Some research suggests a link between food insecurity and reduced physical activity (Gulliford et al, 2006).

The impact on school-aged children has mainly been reported by teachers and children themselves. A study conducted by Chefs in Schools (2022) stated that 88 per cent of teachers who witnessed children coming to school hungry reported that they were tired, with 84 per cent claiming that they were not able to attend to their learning as a result. The National Education Union (NEU, 2023) asked 18,000 of their members about children's hunger and learning, with 87 per cent responding that they had seen children arrive at school tired or unable to concentrate because of a lack of food. In O'Connell et al's (2019a) qualitative study of children's experiences of food insecurity, some reported having to rest their head on their desks at school as they were so tired due to hunger. Research suggests it is long-term lack of food and nutrients that has a lasting impact on children's ability to learn: children with stunted growth, an indication of inadequate food intake over a long period of time, perform poorly on cognitive functioning tests regardless of how recently they have eaten (Lopez et al, 1993). However, when children who typically ate a balanced adequate diet were tested after skipping breakfast for one day, their cognitive functioning appeared to be unaffected (Kral et al, 2012).

The impact of family stress

Alongside these physiological effects of hunger on cognition is the role of family stress caused by a lack of food. The impact of food insecurity on mental wellbeing and family functioning is well documented (Ward & Lee, 2020). Parents experiencing food insecurity often report feelings of guilt and shame about their inability to feed their children, stress from constant financial worries, frustration over limited food options, stigma associated with using food banks, and overall sadness about their situation (Leung et al, 2022). Parents mentioned coping mechanisms such as excessive sleeping or alcohol misuse to manage the persistent stress. Additionally, concerns about the quality and nutritional value of food they can provide contribute to further feelings of shame and guilt (Lindow et al, 2022). Unsurprisingly, these emotions contribute to mental health issues such as depression, stress and anxiety (Pourmotabbed et al, 2020).

Poor mental health among parents is associated with strained family relationships, harsher punishments and reduced responsiveness (Brown et al, 2020; Ward & Lee, 2020). Consequently, food insecurity can alter family dynamics and impact on children's own wellbeing. Children experiencing food insecurity are more likely to suffer from anxiety (Weinreb et al, 2002; McLaughlin et al, 2012) and mood disorders, including depression (McLaughlin et al, 2012; Ke & Ford-Jones, 2015); even though they are less likely to miss meals than their parents, who reduce their own consumption to ensure that children can eat (O'Connell et al, 2019a). The correlation between living with food insecurity and mood disorders may be that stress, anxiety and depression from parents 'trickles down' to children (Dunifon & Jones, 2003). Depression and stress in parents can lead to more negative parent–child interactions which are less warm and nurturing, and this in turn can promote low mood and anxiety in children (Zaslow et al, 2009). This research is all relevant to our discussion in later chapters of the impact on food banks on both children and the wider family.

Food bank research: the critique of neoliberal solutions to poverty

Although our research is focused on schools, we found in our review of the literature on food banks a number of key insights which helped us to contextualise the growth of food banks in schools. There are distinctive differences between food banks in schools and what we term public food banks, which are largely forms of provision that require a voucher to access. Most public food banks in the UK are run by the Trussell Trust, a network of not-for-profit franchises (Lambie-Mumford, 2017). They provide emergency food parcels for people to take home (in contrast to a 'soup kitchen'), and have become emblematic of poverty during the 2010s (Wells & Caraher, 2014; Cloke et al, 2017). Food banks differ from food pantries in that the latter usually require a fee and/or membership, and then users can select their food. As we see in later chapters, some schools run their food provision on this basis, but we use the term 'food bank' to cover all forms of provision. Many food banks rely on the provision of surplus food through organisations such as FareShare and the Felix Project, which redistribute food which cannot be sold, and thus there is an environmental benefit too (Lambie-Mumford & Loopstra, 2020). This approach is presented by organisations as a 'dual purpose' solution, solving two problems at once, but critics fear that this represents giving 'left over food' to 'left over people', reframing the surplus as 'edible waste' and the effect as reducing supermarkets' disposal costs (Riches, 2020).

A further term which requires definition is *food insecurity*. This term is sometimes used interchangeably with food poverty, though this then raises questions about the distinction between food poverty and simply poverty (Lambie-Mumford, 2017). We use the term 'food insecurity' here in keeping with the widely used definition from Anderson: 'Food insecurity exists whenever the availability of nutritionally adequate and safe foods or the ability to acquire acceptable foods in socially acceptable ways is limited or uncertain' (Anderson, 1990, p 1560, cited in Lambie-Mumford, 2017, p 17). This emphasis on social acceptability is important in understanding the complexity of food insecurity; accessing food through a food bank is not a 'socially acceptable' way of acquiring groceries. This is one of the key insights from the food banks literature which we use in this book, which we will discuss. The other key points relate to the concept of deservingness, the depoliticisation of poverty through food banks, and the complex relationships between those who work or volunteer in food banks and those who use them.

Social interactions and food

As noted in Anderson's definition, food has a social dimension; receiving free food from an organisation, even where this is 'surplus food', is not the normal way of acquiring food. Despite the normalisation of food banks, acquiring food in this way remains noticeably 'Other' and can be highly stigmatising (Purdam et al, 2015; Garthwaite, 2016b). Extensive research has found that visits to food banks can be 'deeply stigmatising experiences that already have harmful effects on self-esteem' (Pybus et al, 2021, p 23); Power et al (2020) refer to 'a corrosive sense of shame'. This means that many food-insecure families do not use one; thus, food bank use in England is a 'poor proxy' for food insecurity (Pybus et al, 2021). Pybus et al conclude that 'most people who are food insecure do not visit food banks' (2021, p 35). This reflects international findings that families only use food banks in the most extreme circumstances (Loopstra & Tarasuk, 2012, 2015).

Food insecurity cannot be separated from wider poverty, but has particular consequences. A key point is that within family finances, food costs are more flexible than many other costs such as rent and bills, and thus families may adapt what and how much they eat based on how much money they have left (Graham & Fenwick, 2022). Access to cheap food is also variable, as some areas do not have large supermarkets, and these may also be areas with higher housing and transport costs (Pybus et al, 2021). Food is a particularly sensitive issue, and not having enough has social and emotional consequences, including for children. Purdham et al (2015) note that for their research participants a food bank visit 'involved overcoming considerable embarrassment about being seen as not being able to provide for themselves and their family'. Social research has emphasised the importance of food within families as a source of bonding and the particularities of food insecurity in social as well as health terms (Knight et al, 2018; O'Connell et al, 2019b). Food has a role in defining people's identities; it has cultural and sometimes religious significance, as well as being seen as a basic need which parents need to provide for their children. As Strong comments: 'What we eat signifies more than just a fuel, just as bodies are more than machines' (2019, p 2).

The impact on people's self-worth is linked in some research to the lack of choice available at a food bank (Purdam et al, 2015). There is an expectation, including among food bank workers and volunteers, that users should be grateful for what they are given, as though choosing what you eat is a luxury only afforded to the affluent (Garthwaite, 2017). This negative discourse about lack of gratitude is linked to discourses of deservingness.

The deserving/undeserving poor trope

Within the research on food banks, a common finding is the prevalence of the trope of a division between the deserving and undeserving poor. Within this framing, some of those in need of a food bank are worthy of help, while others are not, often because they have failed to help themselves. Tarkiainen (2022), in her discussion of representations of 'deservingness', points out the long history of discourses of division between those who deserve help and assistance and those who do not, and the continued significance of these in contemporary policy making: '[T]hroughout modern British history, undeservingness has re-emerged repeatedly in different political circumstances but with basic structure unchanged, that is, associating undeservingness with a mixture of physical and mental laziness, irresponsible childbearing, substance abuse and with the inability to defer gratification' (Tarkiainen, 2022, pp 2–3). Importantly, the idea of deservingness 'deals with the obligations and norms related to generosity and conditionality' (Tarkiainen, 2022, p 102). The current norm is that food banks are usually something that you need to be eligible for, as evidenced by production of a voucher (Garthwaite, 2016a). This conditionality does not apply at school food banks, as we see in later chapters, but this does not mean that the idea of a divide between those who deserve help and those who do not disappears. What Tarkiainen (2022) refers to as a continuous performance of the discourse of deservingness rhetorically positions some families as failing to make the most of what they are offered in terms of free food. Those who complain about the choice or amount of food given are regarded as ungrateful and undeserving.

The construction of deservingness currently in play is based on neoliberal processes of individualisation, where each person is responsible for themselves. Use of this deficit framing is exacerbated by the statements from some politicians suggesting the growth of food banks is simply due to greater availability (Garthwaite, 2017), despite the evidence that most food bank use is a last resort. This political argument about what drives the growth of food banks as a solution to food poverty is the next key point from this literature.

The withdrawal of the state and rise in governmentality

As noted in the introductory chapter, there is a range of scholarship internationally on food banks which focuses on their role in depoliticising the problem of poverty, through the removal of this burden from the purview of the state. The US and Canada, where food banks have a longer history, provide evidence of how food banks undermine 'the state's obligation, as ratified in international conventions, to respect, protect and fulfil the human right to food' (Riches, 2002, p 648). As the state withdraws from social welfare obligations, charitable groups and civic society step in to provide food, and the responsibility for hunger shifts to this sector rather than government. Thus, food banks in various forms produce state 'detachment and deniability of responsibility in relation to social welfare and food provision' (Livingstone, 2017, p 2).

This argument has been applied to the UK context, where the growth of food banks in the 2010s is seen similarly as evidence of a denuded welfare state, where reductions in welfare benefits have allowed poverty to grow to a level where people need to access free food (Lambie-Mumford & Dowler, 2014; Dowler & Lambie-Mumford, 2015; Lambie-Mumford & Loopstra, 2020). This is considered by some through the lens of the human right to food, as defined by the United Nations Universal Declaration of Human Rights, in order to question the 'roles and responsibilities of the state and charitable sector when it comes to preventing and protecting people from poverty and food insecurity' (Lambie-Mumford, 2017, p 4).

A further area of discussion is the way that food banks represent a shift in values, as well as practical solutions, when it comes to managing the problem of poverty. As Cloke et al comment, some scholarship from a political economy perspective argues that 'food banks can be seen as inextricably entwined within a multiplicity of largely aggressive political forces deployed to replace established models of welfare provision and state regulation with a free-market fundamentalism that normalizes individualistic self-interest, entrepreneurial values and consumerism' (2017, p 706). For some, this represents neoliberal governmentality; Power argues that state withdrawal cannot be ignored, but that there should be a greater emphasis on 'the transformation of public, social and cultural life according to the principles of the market: competition, entrepreneurship, audit and regulation' (Power, 2022, p 33). This relation to values is important in that the idea of the individual as solely responsible for themselves underpins the withdrawal of the state from responsibility for feeding families, but fails to account for the caring nature of those who respond. Drawing on a Foucauldian analysis of biopower, Strong argues that food banks reveal a 'state that is not only retreating financially from provisioning, but also from the responsibilities for the vital politics that accompany acts of provisioning', that is, from responsibility for ensuring people live (2019, p 1). These analyses align closely with our argument in relation to the responsibilisation of schools, in terms of the withdrawal of the state; however, in our analysis, the individual responsibility reinforced by food banks is alleviated by the school, who step in to solve the immediate problem of family hunger. This represents something distinctive about food banks in schools as opposed to in the community. We return to this discussion in later chapters.

Critiques of the 'Good Samaritan' narrative

Just as the literature on food banks suggests a complex impact on users, the research on those who work or volunteer in food banks is also ambivalent. In particular, there is a critique of a narrative of the 'Good Samaritan' who feeds the poor, as this is seen as an over-simplification of the role of food banks within a neoliberal state. Power argues that food bank organisations' presentations of their work 'do not admit the role which food aid may play in creating stigma, upholding inequalities, and maintaining the very status quo which food charities claim, in public statements and campaigns, to reject' (2022, p 1). While it may benefit organisations to present themselves as helping the needy in terms of donations, this fails to recognise the more negative consequences of food banks and the depoliticisation of hunger as an issue.

At a more local level, ethnographic work in food banks has provided evidence of how workers pathologise the 'food poor', and there are divisions within the food bank users based on who is stigmatised as struggling due to personal failings (Power et al, 2020). Garthwaite (2016b) found some food bank users were seen as engaging in 'faulty behavioural practices' such as spending their money on alcohol or cigarettes rather than food. Because of these relations, there is limited potential for food banks to be spaces of emancipation where new political narratives can be constructed; this is precluded by 'institutionalised classism and the, related, neoliberal narratives of deserving/undeserving poor' (Power et al, 2020, p 919).

However, there is an alternative viewpoint arising from social geography which questions the dominance of the argument that food banks 'depoliticize issues of poverty by institutionalizing food poverty as deserving of charitable emergency aid rather than collectivist welfare entitlements' (Cloke et al, 2017, p 704). While they have sympathy with this view, Cloke et al point out that this focus might obscure more progressive possibilities, and instead suggest alternative ways of 'conceptualizing food banks as spaces of care … introducing values other than neoliberal capitalism' (p 704). The food bank may be a space for 'meaningful encounters between people of different social positions' (p 708). This more hopeful analysis suggests that, particularly where there are no conditions attached to attendance, food banks can be 'investments in compassion that dissolves boundaries' (p 710). Similarly, other scholarship emphasises the possibility of food banks as places of morality, sociality and care, including the work of Williams et al (2016) and Lambie-Mumford (2017), who discuss the moral imperatives for food banks. We return to these perspectives in our final chapter.

Conclusion

This chapter has sought to set out the key insights from our review of the literature on poverty and education; the impacts of austerity and Covid (following our discussion of the cost-of-living crisis in Chapter One); hunger, family stress and learning; and on food banks more widely. While the research reviewed is expansive due to the range of topics covered, we have focused on the key topics which were necessary to contextualise our analysis of the case studies, and particularly those areas which are less familiar to our field of the sociology of education, which has a long history of exploring the relationship between social status and schooling. The key concepts examined here – namely that hunger has complex impacts, that the last decade has had considerable impacts on families and that food banks represent the withdrawal of the state – are areas we return to in the following chapters.

THREE

How do food banks in schools work, and how did they start?

Introduction

Schools and early years settings can be vastly different, with many variabilities between a nursery providing places for 30 children and a primary school which hundreds of children attend. This necessitates food bank provision on different scales and of different types. This chapter explores how schools supply food to families, including where food comes from and how it is distributed to families. We consider how schools use their knowledge of the local community to decide how food is given out, and the role of choice in affording families dignity. We also explore the 'origin stories' of the food banks, in order to consider in more depth why schools have decided to offer this provision.

Central to this chapter is the concept of policy enactment (Braun et al, 2011; Braun et al, 2012), mentioned in Chapter One, which emphasises the importance of context. We discuss how context guides the operation of a school's food bank, even though a policy is not being enacted in the strictest sense. We see this work as similar to 'crisis policy enactment' where actions are taken due to need in a crisis, and argue that education leaders have been emboldened to respond to the needs of families following the Covid pandemic, when they often had to react in an absence of government policy (Bradbury et al, 2022). Thus, we see how the usual ways of understanding what schools do and why need to be adapted to understand this phenomenon.

How do food banks in schools work?

The standard model for schools operating a food bank was to have a set time and place, usually weekly, when parents could come in and take some food free of charge, without the need to produce a voucher which proved they were eligible. There were variations to this, as we will discuss, which were dependent on schools' knowledge of families' circumstances, the local context and the range of other services available; this underlines the position of schools as experts in the needs of local families, particularly in the aftermath of the Covid pandemic (Harmey & Moss, 2023; Bradbury et al, 2022). It is worth noting that the food banks varied considerably in size, with Rashford Nursery School holding a kitchen cupboard of food to give to families, while Rowntree Primary School received 700kg of food each week and distributed it to an estimated 50 families. The food pantry at Oliver Children's Centre, as discussed, also operated on a different model, as an outside agency ran the food pantry at the site and at other children's centres.

We look in this section at the two main elements of running a food bank – sourcing the food and distributing it. We include in this discussion some of the other goods that schools provided, such as toiletries and clothing, and discuss the 'green' agenda which was important in some cases.

Sourcing food

The school food banks sourced food through collaboration with food redistribution organisations, the use of apps that advertised surplus food, or donations from local businesses and even other families. The local context of the setting was important in determining where food could be sourced from, for example, whether the setting had businesses which could support nearby and how mixed the socioeconomic background of families they worked with was.

The majority of our case study schools received donations from food redistribution organisations such as the Felix Project, FareShare and City Harvest, with some schools given food by more than one of these charities. The Felix Project (nd) explains that their operation 'rescue[s] good surplus food' and delivers it to food banks for 'vulnerable children and families, the homeless, the elderly and those who simply cannot afford to buy regular, healthy food' (Felix Project, nd). Both City Harvest and FareShare function in the same way (City Harvest and the Felix Project in London and FareShare across the UK). Booth Primary School, Oliver Children's Centre, Field Nursery School, Twining Primary School and Rowntree Primary School all used one or more of those organisations, with Lansbury Primary School using a similar local food redistribution charity. As we will discuss further, this helped to ease the stigma attached to the food bank in some cases, because they were reducing food waste.

In most cases, the organisation delivered food in vans to the schools we visited, but staff and volunteers at some schools collected the food. Andrea, headteacher at Lansbury Primary School, stated that she had a large car, so would drive to a distribution centre each week to have two or three pallets of food piled into the car boot. She outlined some of the challenges of doing this:

> I would have literally had to go and root around and find what I needed. And also the physicality. It sounds so pathetic, but of one person – we're a school. We don't have spare staff to do this kind of stuff. At least I am not teaching all day every day. So actually, I can take an hour and a half out – even though it's only in term – to go and

drive there, park up, open my boot, get the two pallets. And it was all heavy stuff – tins – [to] get here.

Some of the challenges around supplying food to families are explored in later chapters, but the time, effort and sometimes physical exertion involved in operating a food bank should not be underestimated throughout.

One variation to this system was at Webb Primary School, where they used an app to collect surplus food:

> We're signed up to this thing called 'Neighbourly', which is a social platform thing ... they also do the surplus food collection, so as soon as supermarkets come up, you can put your name down and choose or like whatever days they've got available. So we do Aldi, Lidl, Marks & Spencer and Getir, you know, the delivery thing. And then we have a bank of volunteers – parent volunteers. And off they go, they get the stuff, bring it back. (Genevieve, Webb Primary School)

This system relied on parent volunteers and some coordination, and so was only possible due to the parent body at Webb who had volunteered to collect food.

The very nature of the food that schools received – food which was surplus in supermarkets, restaurants, wholesalers and so on – meant that the type and quantities of food received varied week to week, with schools receiving little notice of what would be delivered to them. In some cases, this meant that schools could receive large quantities of one type of food which was close to its use by date, or there were problems with storing food such as frozen items safely. As Mark at Booth Primary School commented, 'Some days you just get sent, I don't know, 27 Spanish tortillas that are all going off that day'.

As well as these surpluses, schools could also be sent food which was not adequately nutritious or did not meet the needs of the community they served:

> Today we got those big bags of Doritos, we won't give the children the Doritos so they will go to the families or the staff ... There is kind of a borderline because some of the yoghurts are very, very high in sugar so then you have to make an executive decision about is it OK for them to have it or shall we not, shall we just let the parents decide. (Abigail, Field Nursery School)

For Abigail, the food bank presented the additional obligation of deciding whether food was sufficiently nutritious for children to have access to it; she decides to shift the responsibility from the nursery school to parents. Through the food bank, Abigail has become gatekeeper to some foods for families, causing tensions when families had little food.

The cultural appropriateness of food was also a concern for staff in some schools, particularly those in large cities with a high proportion of children and families from minority ethnic backgrounds attending the setting:

> If we've got meat donations Muslim families will only take halal food so that makes it quite challenging when not everything that comes in is halal ... Sometimes Felix will send us some really random vegetables and our assumption was, well that's OK Bengali speaking families will just use those, they will put those into curries, they will put those into cooking, it will be fine. But that was a massive assumption that isn't totally true. (Michael, Booth Primary School)

As a result of this problem, Stephanie, food pantry manager at Oliver Children's Centre, explained that in addition to their deliveries they also purchased more culturally appropriate food; Stephanie explained, 'we have a real emphasis on the fact that our produce is culturally appropriate ... things like apples and bananas don't fit the bill for everyone'. Being 'more diverse', however, was also more expensive. There were also concerns in relation to the amount of fresh food; Helen, setting leader at Brown Pre-School, explained the problem of receiving a lot of tinned food: 'It's a tricky situation because obviously we don't want to be ungrateful and say actually we'd really appreciate it if you started doing [fresh food], but we're limited to what we can use from them ... We just want them [the children] to eat well.'

In contrast, Grace at Webb Primary School felt that families were well served by the range of food they acquired through the Neighbourly app, explaining 'microwave ready meals, we had loads of – that will be everything from a chicken korma to a full roast dinner'. Similarly, Audrey at Field Nursery School stated that staff were 'really, really happy' with the deliveries from the Felix Project and praised the flexibility and communication of the organisation. Overall, participants were keen to emphasise that they were grateful to receive any food to redistribute to children and families.

However, the nutritional value and cultural appropriateness of food for families are valid concerns and indicative of wider issues around a lack of choice of food for those living in poverty. As Caraher and Furey (2017) state, those on low incomes should be able to source food that is culturally appropriate, to their liking and of high nutritional value. No one should feel compelled to eat food they do not enjoy and is damaging to their health. Thus, while food redistribution was a key part of the operation of many of the school food banks, it was not without its problems. Notably, Felicity, who worked with schools at Felix, commented there was a waiting list of over 150 schools and 'it's massively increased this academic year'.

There are criticisms of the use of surplus food for distribution to those living with food insecurity; Riches (2020) re-labels this food 'edible waste' and argues that society ought to provide better, for example. There are also concerns that these systems benefit large corporations by reducing their waste bills and making them appear socially conscious (Power, 2022); however, we did not hear any of these critiques in our research, as staff were more focused on the problems with the quality and quantity of food.

School staff also told us how a range of local businesses, including supermarkets, charities and even other families at the setting, provided donations. Here, again, we see the importance of context (Braun et al, 2011) in acquiring food, for often it was the serendipity of a school's position that allowed for food to be gathered in such a manner. In some cases, supermarkets provided grants and some direct provision of goods to schools, but several other organisations also helped:

> We have the big supermarkets that are also our support, as well ... We have the church. They are really good when giving us donations, as well ... We are connected to a large bakery company, our local factory here, and when they put donations out in front of their factory they'll give us a call and say 'Right, we've put a load out,' and I normally jump in my car and shoot down there and get some fresh bread for all of our families. (Lesley, Peabody Primary School)

Lesley's comments demonstrate the importance of context for schools: where they were located, the businesses surrounding them and the overall food environment influenced where food could be procured from. In contrast, Helen at Brown Pre-School described how families struggled to access their nearest supermarket. Thus, the local contexts in which schools operated shaped their response to families' need for food, but also guided their decisions about how to acquire food.

There were some other organisations which helped with the provision of food, including charities. At Brown Pre-School, where they had few local food providers, they receive help from a more distant organisation called Vitamin Angels, which was one of the most surprising providers of food. Vitamin Angels is a non-profit organisation based in California, who describe their role as 'working to improve nutrition for pregnant women, infants and young children' by bringing 'essential healthcare to underserved communities' (Vitamin Angels, nd). The charity supplies prenatal vitamin and mineral tablets, and their website showcases their work through videos of women and young children across what appears to be Asia, South America and Africa. However, Vitamin Angels were also supporting Brown Pre-School in the North of England: Helen explained, 'the nurseries said don't give vitamins give fruit, vegetables, it will help the schools, it's an easier way to feed the children ... so we get a weekly Tesco haul, and for each child we get five fruit, five veg, and three protein'. Thus, at Brown Pre-School and also at Dimbleby Nursery in London, Vitamin Angels provided fruit and vegetables both for school meals and so that surplus food (predominantly tinned fruit and vegetables) could be taken home. This reliance on charity is indicative of the move from government-provided welfare to assistance from charities and other organisations (Lambie-Mumford, 2017). However, the involvement of an NGO whose aim is to support public health in 'underserved' communities through providing nutritious food to nurseries in England is nonetheless surprising and indicative of the severity of need in some areas.

Another source of donations to the food banks were other families attending the school or from other provision within the chain of nurseries, and in some cases, school staff. At Dimbleby Nursery, they benefitted from revenue raised by a nursery in a more affluent area within their chain, to support the food bank. Through a quiz night and a raffle, they raised £600 for the food bank. Others discussed the donations to the food bank they received from other families attending their own school, such as at Peabody Primary School, where Lesley commented, 'Our parents are amazing.' Again, this was highly dependent on the community the school served, as Gita at Wilson Nursery explained, they were able to support the unit next door for young mothers and babies as '[m]ost of our families are affluent'. At Webb Primary School, where the parents were involved in the food collection, the diversity of parents was key to their provision: Grace and Genevieve discussed how one family offered them a £1,000 donation which they 'earmarked for more vouchers', while another family were 'in dire straits' at a Christmas event. This mix of socioeconomic status among parents was highly significant in this school, as it allowed the food bank and these additional events to function. In contrast, at Booth Primary School, asking for donations from the families was not possible due to widespread poverty, with few parents able to support the food bank. Headteacher Michael explained, 'we don't feel that we've got enough families with the money to be able to make the donations'. The importance of the situated context is again relevant with regard to the families attending the schools. The local community at Michael's school is a double disadvantage for them – Michael needs to provide more support because of the position of the school in an impoverished area and simultaneously does not have wealthier parents to draw on for assistance.

Finally, at Rashford Nursery School, staff funded the food bank. Naomi explained that 'we've got mixes in the families, we've also got mixes in the staff', but staff recognised they were better off than many families. Again, the context is important, as with early years practitioners working alongside qualified teachers (as required in a maintained nursery school), some staff were earning a high enough salary to be able to donate to the food bank, while other members of staff needed support themselves.

Reduced donations due to the cost-of-living crisis

Whatever the source of their food, with the cost-of-living crisis impacting many families, including some of those who were considered more affluent, some schools commented on reduced donations. The manager at Wilson Nursery explained, 'We have noticed in the past month or so that there is less donations', so they were trying to find new sources of funding.

Even schools which received deliveries from one or more of the food redistribution organisations sometimes reported a reduction in the amount of food donated. Stephanie at Oliver Children's Centre noted that increased demand means 'the amount is having to be distributed out further'. For some, this meant having to reduce the amount of food they could offer, such as at Dimbleby Nursery, where Brenda explained, 'We are not getting as much funding as we used to get.' This caused issues with the parents, as we see in Chapter Five. The decrease in the amount of food available in the food banks highlights one of the difficulties of such support, which is that it is contingent upon individuals or organisations being willing and able to provide it. As Lambie-Mumford (2019) attests, a problem with food charity is that recipients of it have no right, and there is no guarantee of the provision.

Distributing food

Schools used a range of strategies to ensure food reached families in need, based on their in-depth knowledge of the communities they served. This was central to understanding how overt or discreet they needed to be in approaching families who may have needed support and when supplying food, they appreciated the complexities involved and the power relations. As Strong argues, 'acts of producing, disseminating and consuming food demonstrate how acts of power become *embodied* – how the quantities, qualities and types of food provisioned shape vitality and vital capacities and capabilities' (Strong, 2019, p 2, emphasis in original). Here, we explain how schools made the decision to target families or not, before describing how food was then provided in practical terms.

Identifying families in need of support

For some schools, there was no targeted approach; the food bank was widely advertised and families were free to attend and collect food whenever it was needed. This form of universal provision to all school families was often advertised via the school newsletter. Some schools opened the provision up to all local families, as at Rowntree:

> We open the doors at 2:45pm to any families at all. It's not referral basis or anything like that. It's absolutely anybody. And because I'm not using my school budget, I've never been precious about it having to be school families. The vast majority are, but we do have some that are just around about in the estate, or they might have heard at other schools. (Charlotte, Rowntree Primary School)

The food pantry at Oliver Children's Centre was also widely available, with the only limitation that it was for families and pregnant women:

> We advertise anywhere and everywhere really. We've got a strong social media presence. We have a weekly newsletter ... we don't do targeting. We also try and avoid any kind of terminology and language that implies that our service is for people that are in need. (Stephanie, Oliver Children's Centre)

Stephanie went on to explain that although the pantry was targeted at 'families who have children under the age of four and pregnant mothers', 'we tend not to discriminate in that if we have other people that turn up and need food, we'll still serve them'. At Booth Primary, they also opened up the food bank to the local community, but it was more common among our sample to focus on the families of children attending the school.

For several schools, there were informal ways of targeting support. For example, at Lansbury Primary School, while the food bank was mentioned in the newsletter, other staff usually pointed parents to the support:

> They [parents] know about it because occasionally we put it on the newsletter, and it's word of mouth ... My [learning] mentor talks to them. And also, we've got a small attendance team. So obviously, they work quite closely together. So if the attendance team are making phone calls and they go, 'We're really struggling, Andrea. We just can't get ...' – that all feeds into the same thing ... We try and say, 'Look, if anybody is struggling, just phone and we'll see what we can do to help.' But there's only a finite amount of food, so that's really difficult. (Andrea, Lansbury Primary School)

This form of targeted support allowed the schools to focus their finite resources on those families most in need. This was one of the key advantages of the food bank at a school, that staff were able to identify who needed support. The headteacher, Michael, at Booth Primary explained: 'I think as schools we can do it in a dignified way, we can also identify the families. The food bank almost relies on a self-referral in a way, whereas we can target the families and we can signpost and target the right families.' This knowledge of the families was vital in the operation of the food banks, and as we see in later chapters, was also strengthened by the relationships built up during visits.

A slightly more difficult issue was the role of the class teacher in identifying children who needed help; these teachers see the children more regularly, but may not feel as comfortable highlighting welfare concerns as the school attendance officer or a family support worker, for example. One teacher explained how it worked at Twining Primary:

> We also, as a class teacher, if I identify somebody ... for example, I had a child come in recently ... they are really on the breadline. So Sarah [head] didn't know anything about them, we didn't have any communication with the other school and [they] moved around a lot. But they needed to access the food bank, so it's kind of

we're referring them and vice versa. She'll come up to me sometimes and say, 'Have you heard anything, what's happening there?' Because more information about a family, the better. (Sophie, Twining Primary School)

Staff thus exchanged details regarding children's learning, attendance and safeguarding factors to build a more complete picture about the family and whether they needed support from the food bank; this became part of the general support for families. Similarly, at Rashford Nursery School, Nicola explained how children presenting as hungry would sometimes alert them to which families needed help: 'Some parents are quite embarrassed about it. So if we're sitting down and we're taking note of the children, how much they're actually eating, so then we can say to the parents, "Do you need a little bit of help? We can help you."' The role of food in the nursery school, where children eat in the presence of staff, enabled staff to identify who was hungry. This is a difference between schools and early years provision, which makes it easier for those working in nurseries to identify hungry children.

Some schools targeted food at families who had requested support. Again, these systems had been developed with an understanding of local families, and were perhaps enabled by the wider discourse around the cost of living:

The plan is that they send an email into the office and all it has is 'School Support' in the title and that's it. And then, myself or one of the Inclusion Team would ring that parent and say 'We've got this email through. This is totally confidential, what can we do to help?' … Normally, once you get to know your family, there is a lot more you can do for them but they just don't want to ask straight away. So it's about building that relationship with our families, knowing what their need is. (Lesley, Peabody Primary School)

> We've found over this winter that parents come to us and it's almost like, 'Oh, I've got no food in the cupboards now.' We hold food bank vouchers, so we do refer to the food banks locally ... But also, we say '[H]ere's a couple of bags of food to keep you going over the next couple of days until you can get to the food bank.' (Naomi, Rashford Nursery School)

Naomi and others at Rashford Nursery School highlighted the close relationships between staff and parents that enabled families to reach out for support in that way. At Peabody Primary, Lesley discussed how 'proud' the families were and how many of them were reticent in asking for help, which was the basis of the email system set up at the school through which families could ask discreetly for food. As we discuss throughout our analysis, the issue of avoiding stigma was important in how food banks were organised.

The different approaches that schools took to identifying families in need and their different numbers of children led to vast differences in the numbers using the food bank. At Rashford Nursery School, the headteacher described providing food parcels to five families, whereas at Rowntree Primary School there were approximately 50 families using the food stall each week. Most staff stated that between 25 and 35 families attended a weekly food bank. This is greater than the number found in a similar study conducted by Baker (2023), which possibly indicates the increase in poverty and food insecurity. As Baker observed, a deep comprehension of the families they worked with enabled staff to tailor food aid to their needs, with an understanding of the shame and stigma sometimes associated with food bank use (Purdam et al, 2015; Beck & Gwilym, 2020).

Ways of distributing food: choice and dignity

As noted, attending a food bank is deeply stigmatising for many users, and key decisions about how the food bank is organised help to alleviate the shame and indignity of receiving free food. Choice is key to a sense of dignity and normality, supporting users to feel like other consumers who can select the food they wish (Garthwaite, 2016a). Most schools established the food bank in a manner that allowed parents to peruse products and select those appropriate to their own needs and likes:

> It's like going into a shop. They go round and then they take what they need and it's nice, and it's done very – 'subtle' is the wrong word, but they're not there in front of everybody. Some schools with the Felix, they put it out on tables in the playground. This is very discreet – that was the word I was looking for – this is very discreet, because our parents are quite proud and to ask for help, it's taken a long time for them to develop that trust and get that relationship going. (Sasha, Twining Primary School)

> It's in the mobile classroom on the other side of the Year 6 classroom … we used to have it out as like a market stall out the front there, and kids would come round and come and see it and stuff … We advertise it in that way, and it's just you know, 'Come along and bring a bag.' (Catherine, Rowntree Primary School)

This approach, these school leaders decided, was the most appropriate for their communities. At several of the early years settings, the smaller-scale provision was always open. Dimbleby Nursery chose to position their food bank in an entrance way, ensuring that families could utilise it at their discretion when taking children to and collecting them from nursery. Similarly, at Brown Pre-School and Wilson Nursery, food was positioned to aid access and the food bank was always open. These settings provided choice of both what to take and when to take it, as well as attempting to maintain some discretion. This was possible usually due to the smaller number of families involved.

In primary schools, parents typically enter the buildings less than in early years settings, usually dropping children off outside a classroom, and this meant that some schools had to find other ways to be discreet. Twining Primary School had gone to great lengths to ensure that the families using the food bank were not seen by teachers or other staff, using a separate entrance:

> So we have a room that's set up downstairs, ready to go, and the way it's positioned, it keeps confidentiality. Families find that very difficult because staff may see them coming in and out, and they don't necessarily want their child's teacher to know that they're struggling a little bit, for whatever reason. So the way that it's set up, it helps to keep that confidentiality. (Sarah, Twining Primary School)

Again, the material context of the school was central to them being able to supply food in this way: Twining Primary had a room available for the food and other items to be placed in. Other interviewees also spoke of the space they had available, often thanks to empty classrooms due to falling rolls or children's centres that had lost funding, to facilitate the food bank being operated in such a way.

The provision of choice was not always possible, and some provided food parcels prepared by staff. This was typically the case in schools where the food bank was smaller or used on a more ad hoc basis when parents requested support:

> I might need to have a private conversation with them and say 'Look, if you're ever in that situation, you just let me know and you can have a bag that day.' We normally give something like a shower gel or soap or some kind of deodorant or something, we would do pasta, soup, vegetables, a pudding, some biscuits, normally a drink like squash or something like that ... And we also try and put something in that they could make together so

like a fajita pack ... Or baking; we'd put cake mix in or something like that so that they can do something together. (Lesley, Peabody Primary School)

Us having food on-site means if we even get a sense of, like, they're struggling, we literally put food in a bag and say, 'Look, take that home.' (Naomi, Rashford Nursery School)

Further limits to choice were sometimes due to the finite amount of food and the need to ensure everyone was provided for. This could be a cause of significant stress for staff, and resulted in strategies to give parents quotas for how much they could take:

There was this one day we ran out. It was horrific. So then we were – I was literally stood there and there was hardly any – there was like some green beans and just – it was awful, and we weren't even halfway through the queue. And hungry people can be angry people as well ... So we do now have signs on some things that say, 'Two of these. Three of these' ... But if we've gotten well through the queue and it still looks like there's quite a lot left, I just shout at everybody, 'Come back round again.' (Charlotte, Rowntree Primary School)

Similarly, at Oliver Children's Centre, they had limits on each item; Stella explained: 'They say, "Can I have two cucumbers instead of one?" I said, "No. One for everyone."' These descriptions of restrictions to ensure fairness indicate that choice can be limited even within a system that promotes it. The issue of choice relates to dignity here, as some families are told they cannot have two cucumbers, for example, making this a very different way of accessing food.

A final alternative strategy was to operate the food bank as a 'food club' or 'food pantry', where parents paid a fee to join and/or a set fee for the food. This was the case at the food pantry element of the provision at Booth Primary, and a similar strategy was used at the food pantry at Oliver Children's Centre, where for £2.50 parents could choose five portions of fruit and vegetables and then five other food items. The manager explained that 'we pride ourselves in being able to give people the choice and selection', but as we have seen, there are limitations on that choice. But many families on low incomes are used to lack of choice; as Garthwaite comments: 'For people coming to the foodbank, though, choice is not something they are likely to be used to', as they have no choice about their benefits or lack of transport, or surviving on 'cups of coffee or tea laced with sugar in place of meals' (Garthwaite, 2016a, p 79). This removal of choice from people takes away their agency and sense of dignity (O'Hara, 2015; Garthwaite, 2016a); these schools were attempting to alleviate this loss through various strategies. We return to the attempts to reduce stigma in Chapter Five.

Non-food provision

At all the case study schools, it was not simply food that was provided, but a range of other goods, to varying extents. Most of the staff informed us that they also supplied hygiene products to families, often supported by external organisations:

> We now also receive support from the Hygiene Project. So we have a hygiene bank as well, so just deodorant, soap, basics, toothbrush, and toothpaste. We've definitely over the last six months noticed a real increase in the number of families that are using it and are coming in and asking for certain things, like toilet roll ... We were speaking to one of the mums who told us that she goes into McDonald's each day to take toilet roll, because she can't afford toilet roll at home. (Bethany, Dimbleby Nursery)

> We're trying to constantly make connections with other charities as well, for example, like Bloody Good Period [a charity providing period products]. We're trying to make connections with them as well, so as well as having those food pantry resources we also have other things. We've got some soaps that they can use as well so it definitely does help. (Gabrielle, Wilson Nursery)

The inclusion of sanitary items at Wilson Nursery demonstrates the extent to which the support was for the family rather than the children, as these were goods clearly not needed by the children. Bethany's comment also reveals the very real need for these products among families who are struggling. Clothing was also often provided to families:

> It started off as non-perishable goods and then we added on the toiletries and then we added on the clothes. And then we had a TA who, basically, had all these brand-new coats, didn't she, that had never been worn that her neighbour had donated to her from a shop. (Lorraine, Peabody Primary School)

> We're going to make a clothing bank because we get donated a lot of clothes, so I've got this idea, it's in progress, that if they want to parents can donate clothes that their children have grown out of which will go into the clothing bank and then they can access bigger clothes. (Abigail, Field Nursery School)

Most of the clothing and shoes offered were for children, although some food banks had adult clothing too. Other household goods were sometimes provided:

> The main source of clothing now is from my 84-year-old parents who are very active in their church. And everybody at their church says, 'Oh, we've got some stuff

> for Andrea's school.' And they're coming today at 12:30 to drop off a load, for example. And that is everything – toys, plates, dishes – basically people have clear-outs and they donate it. We do get a few other donations of bags of clothes and staff will do it a little bit. (Andrea, Lansbury Primary School)

> So word has got out though that we will take household goods. The only thing I don't take is electrical items, because I can't get those checked. (Sarah, Twining Primary School)

Baby equipment was also commonly distributed: for example, at Peabody Primary School, a range of items for families with babies and household goods were placed in a cupboard alongside the food. Again, this reveals how support goes beyond helping the child, and extends to the whole family. As we see in later chapters, the provision of certain items such as clothing and shoes was significant in helping children living in poverty to participate in school life.

The 'green' agenda: cloaking poverty?

As mentioned, for some schools, the need to provide a food bank to alleviate food insecurity and hunger among children and families was accompanied by a desire to support sustainability. Most were very keen to avoid food waste and, in some cases, described going to some effort to ensure the food that was delivered to their setting was used:

> One of the things we also try is to reduce food waste as much as possible here, so if there are things left over at the end of distribution we will look at what we can then use to cook with in the school kitchen, or then it will get redistributed. So I will often end up with either I bring my car here or someone will drop it at my house

and from there I distribute from mine to a number of foster families that live near me or some other homeless projects and so on. There is an added bonus in that the food that's left over from our food pantry then always gets to another good home elsewhere, or staff will use it, I'll use it, whatever, to make sure it doesn't go to landfill. (Michael, Booth Primary School)

I am quite environmentally conscious so I do enjoy kind of using vegetables that sometimes are given to us and most people would go, 'Well that's unusable', and throw it in the bin. (Greg, Wilson Nursery)

This desire to avoid food waste was not a dominant feature of provision for most of our schools, as most were solely focused on alleviating food insecurity; it was simply another thing to bear in mind. For others, the sustainability agenda supported them in encouraging families to use the food bank:

At first they didn't really want to take it they were like, give it to somebody that needs ... and we're like 'Either you guys take it or it's going to go in the bin', and they're like, 'If it's going to go in the bin we'll take it.' (Audrey, Field Nursery School)

I feel like it's a bit different these days, like people aren't as ashamed. Because we also sell it as though 'come and save the planet'. (Genevieve, Webb Primary School)

Presenting use of the food bank as a means to avoid food waste and therefore promote sustainability encouraged more families to take food in some of the schools visited. At Webb, this was an important part of the food bank, as the food was collected from supermarkets and the entire enterprise was painted as a 'green' project. The model of the food redistribution charities is to highlight the benefits for the environment alongside the improved wellbeing of food bank users. The Felix Project website calls attention to the fact that it saved 34,021 tonnes of carbon dioxide from being emitted into the atmosphere in 2023, as well as distributing enough food to provide 32 million meals (Felix Project, nd).

However, it is important to consider if emphasising such gains for sustainability obscures the problem of food insecurity and poverty. Baker (2023) discusses the way in which schools presented food charity as a 'food pantry' or 'community shop' to minimise food waste and therefore avoid the stigmatising term 'food bank'. Caraher and Furey (2017) argue that linking surplus food and the reduction of food waste to resolving food insecurity and hunger means that full attention is paid to neither and that neither goal is achieved. Furthermore, it removes the political impetus to focus on the problem of food insecurity: 'There is evidence from other countries that the use of surplus food for emergency food aid "depoliticises" hunger and allows governments not to address the gap between income and food costs' (Caraher & Furey, 2017, p 1). We return to this issue of depoliticisation in Chapter Six. We now turn to the reasons why families were using food banks.

How did food banks in schools start?

Understanding how the food banks in schools developed is key to conceptualising them as a response to poverty. We focus here, as mentioned in Chapter One, not on the reasons why child poverty has increased, but more on the reasons why schools have begun to help. Our case study schools discussed setting up a food bank in response to the impact of one of three challenges – the austerity policy during the 2010s, the Covid pandemic in 2020–21 or the cost-of-living crisis from the end of 2021 onwards. Notably, the typical pattern was that food provision was set up either before or during the Covid pandemic, but that schools had recently seen use increase due to the cost-of-living crisis.

While the Covid pandemic drew attention to the issues of child poverty and food insecurity, austerity measures taken by successive governments between 2010 and 2019 were a major factor, as discussed in Chapter Two. Field Nursery School, Twining Primary School and Booth Primary School had all initiated a supply of food for families prior to the pandemic. Staff in those schools all described piecemeal provision that was widened when Covid hit:

> Before Covid we were working a bit with the Felix Project and we were doing some real ad hoc food distribution, a little bit here and there each week. Felix would bring a donation in and we'd distribute it just in the playground but not to any targeted audience and just it was a very small amount so we didn't really recognise that as a great need. And then when Covid came the need became more and more apparent. (Michael, Booth Primary School)

> So pre-Covid, so say 2019, I had seven families that were using it regularly, and most of those were no recourse to public funds, so they were caught in the immigration system ... then that first big lockdown we had, that trebled literally overnight. (Sarah, Twining Primary School)

For these schools, what had been identified as a key need in the 2010s increased during the Covid crisis. Many of the schools that started a food bank due to the impact of the pandemic described doing so at the beginning of the first lockdown, with the supply of food to families a primary concern:

> It started with Covid. So the day that Boris Johnson said he was closing schools, we closed for one day and only one day completely, because my very first fear was about food for our families, before learning and before anything

else. So after one day our kitchen staff and one or two other staff agreed to come in. And this is really early days when it was very frightening and everything, and we just baked lots of jacket potatoes and we had cheese and tuna and things. And we went out and we put a table across the school gate and just said, 'If anybody needs lunch, anybody in the family, it doesn't matter how many, just come down and get a jacket potato.' And that was the very first thing, and it grew from there. (Charlotte, Rowntree Primary School)

During the initial lockdown, the Inclusion Team and the headteacher got together and we had to come up with a solution for our families who were really struggling and we decided to create the food bank. So I've been part of that since it was first created and it's just ballooned. (Lesley, Peabody Primary School)

So the [name of organisation] was set up during Covid. We have partnered with [organisation] who had identified a need within [area] and they wanted to be able to support their communities through food better. So that's where we started from. We started initially by doing home deliveries for people, particularly pregnant mothers, and it was grocery bags particularly with fruit and vegetables, but we were also doing a meal prep service ... From there, our pantry model was then curated and we've grown and grown since then. So we've now got five. (Stephanie, Oliver Children's Centre)

This growth during Covid mirrors survey results showing that, in the first two weeks of lockdown, 20.8 per cent of families with children experienced food insecurity (Food Foundation, 2024) compared to 11 per cent between 2016 and 2018 (Sosenko et al, 2019). These comments echo those collected at the time which emphasised the prioritisation of food for many schools (Moss et al, 2020). Many of our participants referred to the loss of employment for many parents as the reason for this increased need for food provision, reflecting research on low-income families during the pandemic (Patrick et al, 2022).

Some practitioners who we spoke to stated that they initially believed the food bank would be a short-term measure to support families during Covid, but the cost-of-living crisis from late 2021 had seen the level of need within their communities continue or even increase:

> We had a lot of families that lost their jobs over Covid, were made redundant so we didn't have the foodbank, our kind of food poverty at that time so we ended up using another local foodbank provider to help support families with that ... It seems to be worse now than it was then. I think it's just crept in, it's crept in slowly and then all of a sudden we've had a huge boom, it's always in conversation with parents, everything is so expensive, food. (Helen, Brown Pre-School)

> I started in September 2021 and the store started here about six months before that, and it's been gradually building since then. Not dramatically but gradually I would say ... Cost of living is going up. Cost of energy, and food in the supermarkets, and markets has gone up. So, people struggle to afford it. (Matt, Booth Primary School)

Similarly, at Oliver Children's Centre, Stephanie commented that 'numbers have gone up' due to the cost-of-living crisis. At Dimbleby Nursery, Bethany noted that 'people that wouldn't have been accessing the food bank this time last year are now'; while Mark, head chef at Booth Primary School, commented on the extra food he needed to order due to increased demand. Sarah, at Twining Primary School, explained how numbers had 'trebled overnight' due to the first lockdown, but went on to say:

> 2021, it started to go down again because obviously things started to open up, once families went back to employment … It started to go up in the October '22. We started to notice that I was getting sort of like two or three more, then three or four, then five or six. It's not been a massive jump, all in one go. It's been spread out over the last few months. But I'm up to between 30 and 35 at the moment. (Sarah, Twining Primary School)

This figure of 35 was compared to seven families needing support before the pandemic.

For some, the cost-of-living crisis was the trigger for opening the food bank. At Webb Primary School, they had previously provided support to families in the form of vouchers during Covid: 'We put a thing out to parents saying, "Hey, we realise the cost-of-living crisis. We're doing this thing. If anybody would like to be on the list to be alerted when we have surplus food, let us know." So we've got a list of about 20 people.'

The experiences of those interviewed correlate with research stating that food insecurity peaked *after* the Covid pandemic, with 25.8 per cent of families affected in September 2022 (Food Foundation, 2024). As noted, the emergence of the cost-of-living crisis in the summer of 2021 coincided with the removal of the £20 a week increase in Universal Credit payments, a policy which in itself is believed to have resulted in 350,000 more children living in poverty (CPAG, 2023). The headteacher at Rowntree Primary explained how her school had tried to reduce the frequency of the food bank following the pandemic, only to find that the demand was still as great:

> We'd gone to fortnightly. Once we really were sort of, well in educational terms anyway, over Covid and

everything else was back to normal, and Ofsted were back on the agenda and testing and everything else, it was like, 'Right, we can't do this every week. It is A) exhausting and B) time consuming. We'll just do it fortnightly.' Oh, no. I think we only managed a few weeks doing it fortnightly before we realised that 'No, the need is there.' (Charlotte, Rowntree Primary School)

As well as overall continuing need, there was a recognition that food insecurity was no longer the reserve of those families with parents who were not working, and that even those who would previously have been considered wealthier were affected by increasing costs and interest rates:

So many single mums that are working in schools that can no longer — as I say, they've got two dependents on one income and then — or maybe three dependents, or four. And then you've got one income, and then you've got your utilities and your food costs. It's a real kind of hot — even if you are a teacher or a doctor or a well-paid job, that's not going to work anymore. (Grace, Webb Primary School)

And the other big thing I've noticed is some of it is working families as well, it's the part-time families and the single mums and single dads, they're the ones that are coming forward a lot more now than would have been before. (Audrey, Field Nursery School)

These comments reflect a wider concern with in-work poverty, and the growing proportion of families struggling during the cost-of-living crisis. There were also concerns about families who had been affected by the unexpected nature of the cost-of-living crisis:

Even if you're really wealthy, you'll still struggle because we didn't know this was coming, this cost-of-living thing.

And people might have over-mortgaged themselves. Like I do see these people pulling up in their big fancy cars and coming to the food bank, but it doesn't mean that they don't need it. Because they probably took out that loan or something before all of this happened, or they might have lost their job or whatever. (Genevieve, Webb Primary School)

A final sign of the impact of the cost-of-living crisis and another reason to run the food bank was the number of school staff using the food bank. Many discussed the discreet measures they took to supply colleagues, mainly teaching assistants and cleaners, with food and other items to support them. This was justified by the need to keep healthy staff in some cases:

> We've got staff that are struggling. We've got staff on minimum wage so as much as we want to help the children and families we do give our staff a lot of food, leftover milk at the end of the week, because they're just — we need to keep them healthy and in the right frame of mind to support these children. (Helen, Brown Pre-School)

> There are a couple of staff members who are really struggling as well so I normally keep a bag of food to the side for them and then give it to them very discreetly to support them as well. (Abigail, Field Nursery School)

The use of the food banks by staff, particularly those in support roles, is perhaps unsurprising given the low pay. In 2019, prior to the Covid pandemic, it was estimated that 14 per cent of nursery staff were living in relative poverty, with roughly 3 per cent needing assistance from food banks (Crown, 2019). Staff use did, however, cause some tensions, as at Rowntree Primary and Wilson Nursery they had to ask staff to take food after the parents otherwise there was not enough, suggesting a high level of need among those working at the school. The difficult decision that leaders made to prioritise families using the food bank demonstrates the emotional cost of running a food bank in an education setting.

Conclusion

This chapter has set out how the food banks in school operate in terms of sourcing the food and distributing it, and the extra clothing, toiletries and other non-food items that schools offer. We have also discussed the green agenda which is present in some schools and explored the reasons why schools first set up food banks in response to record levels of child poverty (CPAG, 2024). Throughout this chapter, we have seen how context matters in the operation of the food bank, in terms of local population, size of buildings, needs of the families and sources of food. How schools perceive this context is also vitally important in understanding how they operate a food bank. This discussion cannot be seen as analogous to policy enactment, however, as the schools are not required to offer a food bank. In fact, they are responding, as we argue in Chapter Six, to *an absence of policy*. Nonetheless, we can see these actions as similar to 'crisis policy enactment' during Covid, where education leaders responded to the needs of their communities in the absence of government policy (Bradbury et al, 2022), prioritising welfare and basic needs, such as food. This leads us onto the discussion in Chapter Four on the benefits of the food bank for both families and the school, and then in Chapter Five to a discussion of how leaders are guided by a moral and ethical obligation to support families in need. We would argue that, for some schools, responding in a more autonomous way to the community during the pandemic has emboldened leaders to meet the needs of children and families in the cost-of-living crisis, regardless of government policy. But this does not entirely explain the continuation of food banks or the ones that began pre-Covid; instead, we need to take into account the wider responsibilisation of civic society and charitable organisations for food insecurity, and include schools within this discussion.

FOUR

What is the impact of food banks on children and their families?

Introduction

In this chapter, we set out the impact of having a food bank in a school or nursery, from the perspective of those who work there. The impact is significant, for many of our participants, but diverse, and certainly goes far beyond an impact on children's learning. We explore in this chapter how adults in various roles perceive the effect of families having regular access to free food on children's learning, participation and motivation, demonstrating that these real-life examples reinforce the wider literature on the relationship between hunger and these important factors in learning. We then discuss the wider social impacts of receiving food and other goods, including how children with donated shoes or clothes that fit them can take part in activities and otherwise 'fit in'. This benefit of being able to experience and enjoy ordinary childhood activities is important in understanding the impact of food banks in schools, and is an area under-explored in the existing literature. Food banks are part of a school's practices of inclusion, in that they allow all children to participate in all aspects of school life.

A third section of the chapter focuses on the impact on families, which is seen by teachers to be far more diverse than simply reducing hunger. Families were seen as enabled to spend money on their heating or other essentials, because they had food, and were seen as having lower stress levels. In this discussion, we also examine how school staff's perceptions of families include some deficit discourses about poor parenting practices, bad choices of food and lack of education. These discourses, we argue, form part of a continued deserving/undeserving poor narrative that remains in education and society more broadly. This points to the complexity of food banks as a social practice, a point which we return to in more detail in our concluding chapter. These comments also show the frustrations felt by some school staff about the effort that is taken to provide food banks and the barriers to having a positive impact. We end the chapter with some more detail on the impact on particular groups of families facing additional challenges, such as those in temporary accommodation due to homelessness. We emphasise here that each school is serving a different community with different needs, and is well placed to understand and cater for these needs, making them an ideal hub for welfare support. The chapter concludes with some comment on the need to understand the full range of impacts on children and their families, despite the research challenges, if we are to understand properly the importance of food banks.

Impact on learning

Concentration and 'brain development'

The impact on learning of having a food bank was an important, but not dominant, point of discussion throughout our data collection. While the literature suggests a strong relationship between children's ability to focus and their hunger levels, and our everyday experiences suggest clear connections between food and concentration, this impact did not seem to be as important to our participants as we expected. We asked specifically about the impact on learning, but found the diversity of impacts meant that participants often talked about many other effects, and had to be asked again about learning (this is perhaps reflective of a broader conceptualisation of learning, present particularly in early years). When prompted, however, the majority of our primary school participants were clear that children who were hungry were unable to learn, and it was the effect of hunger on concentration that was most frequently mentioned:

> But they can't learn if they haven't had anything to eat, can they? ... So lack of concentration is the main one ... It's just not being able to concentrate. You know what it's like when you have nothing to eat and you've got nothing in your belly, you can't concentrate. (Sophie, Teacher, Twining Primary School)

> I think obviously if they're in school and they're feeling hungry then that impacts upon their work and their concentration. They're going to feel unwell. They're going to feel unmotivated. (Martha, Booth Primary School)

> We've had some [children] that maybe haven't had much since lunch at school the previous day. And you can't concentrate on your reading comprehension if you can't – if you're hungry. (Catherine, Rowntree Primary School)

These views are consistent with those voiced by teachers in teaching union surveys (NEU, 2023), and are supported by research demonstrating the impact of hunger on cognitive functions, including concentration (Lopez et al, 1993). Similar points were made in the nurseries: when asked if children were more engaged with their learning, Gita (Wilson Nursery) replied, 'Yeah, definitely because they have full bellies and they can concentrate a little bit better.' For some of the early years staff, this discussion was framed in the language of 'basic needs':

> We expect the children to be coming in and doing all these different things and I just think there's no point in any of it if they're not having their basic needs met first. (Bethany, Dimbleby Nursery)

> It's one of their basic needs to have food, so if we can provide that or if we can help contribute towards providing that in their home environment, it all makes such a big impact on them because they will feel, their basic needs will be met, but they will also feel excited, they will feel happy. They'll feel ready to learn, you know, and they need food, they need all of that nutrition to help them function and to help their brain make those connections that they need, especially at this age, because in the first five years of their life, that's when all of the connections in their brains are happening. (Gabrielle, Wilson Nursery)

This language of 'basic needs' draws on Maslow's Hierarchy of Needs, a theory commonly taught in education courses, which states how children cannot learn if they are cold, scared or hungry (Lester, 2020). Only once these needs are met, can children address other needs, such as learning. Gabrielle's comments also suggest an understanding of the neurological impact of hunger reflecting a wider adoption of neuroscience in education (Busso & Pollack, 2015; Bradbury, 2021). This work often emphasises the importance of the first three years in brain development through the language of 'critical periods' (Bruer, 1999), but has been critiqued for oversimplifying the insights gained from neuroscience for education (Corrie, 2000; Billington, 2017). In these comments, we see a generalised concern for children's growth and development which appears to draw on a range of biological and neurological ideas.

In the early years settings, there were very clear connections made between the children's learning and the free breakfast provided (which participants discussed as part of the overall free provision for families, despite our focus on food banks). Natalie at Rashford Nursery School explained how breakfast 'gives them the boost of energy that they need' so that 'they're now ready to learn'. There were also extensive discussions about the opportunities for learning provided by having breakfast together in the mornings, so that the free provision helped children to develop what Naomi at Rashford Nursery School described as 'independence skills', such as washing their hands, scooping cereal and washing up their bowls. The opportunity to eat together also built social and language skills. Naomi explained, 'lots of areas of the curriculum we can get out of the breakfast. So it doesn't take away from learning time. It's actually used as a learning time.' Similarly, at Wilson Nursery, Gabrielle explained that getting different fruit 'means that they're able to taste and try these things but it also means that we can plan fun cooking activities'. Thus, for the early years staff, the provision of free food at the setting had broader learning benefits beyond simply reducing hunger so that children could concentrate. This is a further example of the different context of early years having an effect on the operation of free food provision, and also aligns with research which suggests food insecurity in younger children can be particularly damaging (Markowitz et al, 2021).

Physical impacts and behaviour

Participants from the primary schools, when asked about physical impacts from having a food bank, were reluctant to make any connection and, perhaps understandably, were unable to identify any impact on children's activity levels. This contrasts with the literature which makes a link between food insecurity and reduced physical activity (Gulliford et al, 2006), but is possibly due to teachers being unaware of levels of physical activity at play time or after school and how they are affected by having a food bank. One participant explained, 'As leaders, we probably wouldn't see that, to be honest. I don't spend much time thinking about PE and we don't do lunch and break duty.' Certainly, none of the primary school participants talked in terms of malnutrition or insufficient nutrients, as they could not know what the children would be like without the presence of a food bank. The impacts of poor nutrition on children may also be only apparent in the longer term (Lopez et al, 1993), as one headteacher commented:

> I don't think that we're yet seeing the impact of it but I think that in time we will. I think we're still seeing children, the levels of inactivity through the Covid period are still having a negative impact, that is improving but it's got a way to go. And I think the food is a big part of that but I think that we're not going to see any impact on that for some time. (Michael, Booth Primary School)

In this school, they regarded the food banks as part of their post-Covid recovery plan, helping children to eat healthily after a period of reduced activity.

Staff in early years settings engaged more with the physical impacts on children, whether this be related to quality or volume of food:

> A lot of the staff have mentioned before when they're eating proper food they notice a difference in the children. They're more energetic. (Helen, Brown Pre-School)

> [If children don't eat] They're just not as energetic as they normally are. They're not as talkative as they normally are. (Nicola, Rashford Nursery School)

Nicola also mentioned how children arrived without having breakfast and would 'become quite lethargic … a bit weak', echoing wider findings (United Nations World Food Programme, 2006). There was one comment on children being underweight:

> You can often tell that the families where they are really struggling food-wise – the children can be quite thin and – so it's definitely – with the food that they get here, they would have plenty of energy to be running around in the playground. We don't seem to have any children who can't engage in all the nursery activities. So I'm sure that the provision of food contributes to that. (Naomi, Rashford Nursery School)

Again, however, physical impacts were not a major reason for having a food bank for the whole family.

Far more significant in both primary schools and the early years settings was the impact on behaviour of having enough food; as Grace at Webb Primary School explained, food 'definitely helps with behaviour and sleep and concentration'.

> So I can't say that I've actually really noticed children being lethargic or not joining in, but definitely notice a difference in the behaviour. (Bethany, Dimbleby Nursery)

> I think without it we would see more behavioural issues and therefore we would be spending more time on children's behavioural issues and I think that that would lead to poor learning. The worst-case scenario is that if we had poor behaviour, poor learning, then that might lead to poor teacher retention and the whole vicious downward spiral starts where then poor teachers leads to even worse learning, leads to even worse behaviour, leads to even worse outcomes, etcetera, etcetera. (Michael, Booth Primary School)

This more noticeable impact on behaviour is important given the significance of behavioural issues – as Michael points out – in the overall functioning of the schools. Dealing with significant behavioural issues reduces the time children spend learning and the time teachers have to teach; as Brenda suggests in her comments about squabbles, which she has to deal with. In some cases, there were also links made between food, behaviour and children's wider wellbeing, to which we now turn.

Children's wellbeing

Well beyond the impact on learning, many participants commented on the positive contribution the provision of free food and other goods made to children's wider wellbeing. Children were happier, many commented, because there was less stress at home. Clear links were made between children's ability to learn, and their levels of stress and anxiety about food:

> [Children] have undoubtedly had things off the food stall for breakfast. And you think, 'Well, yes, you wouldn't be able to concentrate on writing an explanation text would you if you hadn't got that bowl of Shreddies in your belly right now?' … if you're not eating, and you've not got food in the house. I think that phrase food insecurity is really good because it's unnerving isn't it? I mean, that stress and worry of not knowing where your next meal comes from causes an insecurity. (Charlotte, Rowntree Primary School)

Given the instability of some children's home lives, respondents told us about the impact on children's wellbeing and mental health of having more food security at home:

> The last thing a child is going to be able to do is to sit there and concentrate on their work – one, if they're hungry. Two, if they're worried, 'Is Dad coming home tonight? Is he going to start arguing with Mum?'. They've

got all these other sorts of worries and concerns. The last thing they're going to be able to do is to sit and pay attention to a bit of history about Henry VIII and his six wives. It's just not going to happen. (Sasha, Twining Primary School)

This aligns with wider literature on financial insecurity and family stress (Treanor, 2020; Ward & Lee, 2020) which emphasises the connection between worries about food and increased arguments at home. For these participants, the food bank was one bit of security the school could provide to reduce the number of concerns children faced. In one powerful comment, a headteacher described an encounter with a child who had come to her office after receiving food from the food bank:

So he came in all full of beans. 'I've got all gold. Look at my work. Can I have a sticker? ' And I was like, 'Someone's had their Weetabix,' and they're like, 'Yeah, I did. I had that special Weetabix from Genevieve.' And then it turned out the dad had been into the food bank … that's why, that's why I'm doing this. (Grace, Webb Primary School)

Here, the impact on the child's energy level translates into more learning and an opportunity for praise from the headteacher, suggesting an overall positive effect of the food bank on this child.

While there were fewer comments about children being affected by family stress in the early years settings, there was an awareness of the impact on younger children of food insecurity:

That's always going to impact the children in one way or another, isn't it? If you've got a stressful home situation, it's always going to impact the child somehow. Even with the best will in the world, it still will. So some of the children here, especially the older children, are quite aware of their home situation. Even at age 4, they will come and say when they have breakfast, 'I wanted breakfast this morning, but we don't have any food because we don't have any money to get cereal,' and things like that. Or they'll come in, maybe things that the parents wouldn't ask for, the children will come in and say, 'Can I have some of that for at home, for my house?' and things like that. So it definitely does, because it's things that a 4-year-old shouldn't be worrying about. So it definitely does impact the children as well. We definitely do see that. (Bethany, Dimbleby Nursery)

As Bethany notes, children are aware of the lack of food in their homes, and the food bank reduces these concerns which they 'shouldn't be worrying about'. As we discuss in a later section, there is an overall impact on the whole family.

Some participants also discussed the way in which alleviating some of the stress associated with poverty allowed parents to spend more time with their children on activities to support learning. When one staff member at Peabody School was asked if the food bank improves learning outcomes, she asserted:

I think, with a lot of our families, it does have an impact and I don't know whether it's because we're helping the parent with their mental health but then, they can spend that time with their child, reading, in the evening; they're not sitting there worrying about 'I've got to do this, I've got to do that.' Or if you meet the need of the parent, they're then available to meet the need of the child … Whereas before, that parent would be so 'I haven't got food, what am I going to do? What am I going to cook? I need to go and ring someone to get some money or I need to go …' It's taking that away and allowing them to parent. (Lesley, Peabody Primary School)

This aligns with the previous comments on reducing the burden on parents so that they are able to engage with children's learning, and shows how sympathetic many of our participants were about the difficulties faced by some families. We see the intertwined impact of the food bank on learning in terms of concentration, and reducing stress for both parents and children.

Social impacts

As Townsend (1979) stated, a key feature of poverty is being unable to participate fully in society; in these schools, the food bank had an impact of allowing children to participate in both school life and ordinary childhood activities like celebrating Christmas or buying a present for a parent. This impact was more important than we had anticipated; the food bank and wider free provision related to children's ability to participate in everyday activities, which was highly related to their wellbeing.

Being able to join in with all aspects of school life made a huge difference to some children. In particular, participants noted the importance of having uniform which fits and the same uniform as everyone else. Lesley at Peabody Primary School explained the emotional impact of 'fitting in':

> You see the children, if you've given them – they might be wearing an ill-fitted skirt or trousers – we've had children who couldn't even do up their buttons and parents have just used elastic bands to hold them. We've given them pairs of trousers and they've come in – one little girl, she'll come in and she'll swish about: 'Do you like my new skirt?' She doesn't need to know where it's from, just go 'You look amazing!' And she goes 'Yes, that's my new skirt.' And it's that is what you can't really judge on whether that's helping them, academically, but definitely emotionally and mentally, that they're getting

what they need. They're getting the same as everybody else: 'They've all got skirts that fit; now I've got a skirt that fits.'

As Lesley points out, the impact on academic achievement cannot be judged, but there is a clear emotional impact of simply being like everyone else, and having clothes that fit. Similarly, at Rowntree Primary School, the headteacher commented how a boy in Year 6 who had outgrown his uniform was bought an entire new set by the school, and at Peabody School providing uniform allowed a child to belong:

> He's the only one in his class that's not in school uniform ... I got him in, we had tea and biscuits together and we'd been to Tesco, and we'd bought him two brand new pairs of school trousers and then we'd got a new school T-shirt and a new school jumper. Put his name in everything and then after we'd had tea and biscuits I said, 'Right, I've got something for you,' and his little face lit up. (Charlotte, Rowntree Primary School)

> I gave [staff member] a bag, this morning, of uniform with the logo on so that we can make sure that those children have the right uniform. It's really important that it makes them feel part of the school and that they're not on their own. (Lorraine, Peabody Primary School)

Thus, providing free uniform at the food banks was clearly related to children's wellbeing and dignity, and sense of belonging. This was also clear with comments on providing shoes, as in this example of a boy who was bought shoes by the school. As a result, Lesley comments, he experienced the physical and emotional relief of being given shoes that fit him after months of not being able to run in too-small shoes:

> It meant so much more than just getting a pair of shoes. That was he wasn't uncomfortable anymore, he could run around, he could play football, he wasn't embarrassed, he just was the same as everybody else, and I think that's what a lot of them want, just to fit in. (Lesley, Peabody Primary School)

These comments emphasise the widespread and insidious impact poverty can have, if help is not provided; children were able to able to participate in normal school activities, because they had the right clothing and shoes provided by the school. Clothing was also mentioned in the early years settings, although without uniforms this was a less important issue in terms of participation. There were some comments on children who were not well fed being less engaged and more isolated, however, such as Natalie at Rashford Nursery School, who explained, 'they'll just go and do their own thing'. Children who receive free food are able to participate more and experience the social benefits of being at a nursery.

Children's wellbeing was also enhanced by the provision of 'extras' alongside the food bank, which allowed them to access 'normal' childhood experiences and to be fully involved in school life. These 'extras' allowed children to engage in experiences outside of school, such as being able to celebrate birthdays and religious holidays. For example, at Rowntree Primary School, Charlotte explained how she saw the impact of some large chickens that they had given out on their food stall, which allowed a child to feel excited about her Christmas dinner:

> I'd been talking to a little girl, and she was talking about Christmas Day. And I'm always very careful about what I ask about what might happen, but she was looking forward to it. So I said, 'Oh, what are you looking forward to the most on Christmas Day?' and she said,

'Oh, mum's going to cook Christmas dinner.' I was like, 'Oh, wow. What are you going to have then?' She said, 'She's got this massive chicken in the freezer,' and I just thought, 'I know where that's from' … it was just a chicken, but it meant a lot to them. So things – little wins – like that are lovely. They're really nice. (Charlotte, Rowntree Primary School)

Several schools held additional food bank sessions around Christmas time and made a particular effort to ensure that families were not hungry over the holidays. It appeared that staff appreciated that Christmas is a time where food is highly significant in terms of social practices, and they wanted to ensure all children were able to experience this normal event. At Peabody Primary School, they gave children gifts for them to give to their family members, so they could have this experience:

When it's Christmas time, we can go out and give them presents and we watch a child wrap a present and they have no idea how to wrap a present because they've never done it. Again, it's those life skills: 'Actually, we're teaching you, this is what you do, this is how good it feels to give a little present' … And they will say about ten times to their class teacher, 'Don't let me forget my gift, don't let me forget my gift.' And then, when they take it out, they're like 'Mummy!' And that is why we do what we do because that child would not have that experience if we didn't provide that for them. (Lesley, Peabody Primary School)

Similarly, in the early years settings, additional extras such as clothing and toys were provided at Christmas time to help children experience a 'normal' Christmas. Other events such as World Book Day were a concern, so at Peabody School they also provided costumes:

> I think it's just allowed them to feel part of the community and it's allowed … for example, if we hadn't have given out World Book Day costumes, would those children have come to school that day? Possibly not because their parents wouldn't have wanted them to feel left out of things. (Lorraine, Peabody Primary School)

These activities suggest a broader awareness of the impact of poverty on what might seem normal everyday activities; free provision allowed children to fit in, and have dignity, and to experience what many families take for granted as part of childhood. Thus, we would argue that food banks are part of a school's practices of inclusion because they allow all children to participate in school life. This is an area which has not been explored in the existing literature thus far, and certainly one which could be explored in more depth.

Impact on families

Family wellbeing

The wellbeing of the child and their wider family are clearly interlinked, as we have seen in comments about reducing family stress due to food insecurity. The impact on the wider family of the food banks was clear in comments about children's parents and siblings, who were seen as also the concern of the school:

> I know mums that haven't eaten, mums that have lost weight, and mums that can't afford to buy – so they put the children first. I've had children tell me, 'My mum doesn't eat. We have tea, but she doesn't eat. She goes into the other room. She says she eats later, but I know she doesn't.' And I've talked to mums, and that's definitely what's happening with some of them. (Charlotte, Rowntree Primary School)

> One of the mums recently was so happy that a certain milkshake was on offer in Asda. So she bought a load because she said, 'A lot of the time, I can't afford for me to have dinner as well, but at least then I know if I've got them in the fridge, I can have a milkshake.' So I think a lot of it is just that they go without rather than getting help. (Bethany, Dimbleby Nursery)

These comments reflect those earlier about children worrying at a young age about food, and with wider findings on the impact of poverty on children which demonstrate the multifaceted impact as parents worry about their children, reduce their consumption, and then children worry about their parents (O'Connell et al, 2019a). The staff were acutely aware of how much stress parents were under due to food insecurity, and how this affected children:

> Sometimes even just getting them out the door to go home, the fact they have something, they have an option there. But also, you know, a lot of them are probably thinking 'What do I cook today?' Or 'What can I provide, what is something quick that won't take a lot of hassle?' And they have that option there by using it. (Gabrielle, Wilson Nursery)

> Just by some of the reaction that you get from parents when you give them stuff, and it's – you can almost see parents just going – almost taking a [breath] – you know, their shoulders go down, they can – 'Oh right, I can make a meal tonight.' Because at the end of the day, our parents are good parents. They want to – they do prioritise their children. If they are struggling for food, the children will eat and they won't. So that actually – that's not great for the parents' wellbeing. And if the parents' wellbeing isn't good, it does have an effect on the children. The children

sense the atmosphere and the strain. (Naomi, Rashford Nursery School)

In these cases, the school's concern was for the impact on the child, but also independently for the parents, suggesting a feeling of responsibility for the entire family. Having food to provide allows the staff to alleviate parents' stress. We were also told about more severe cases (which we do not quote here for reasons of anonymity) where food insecurity contributed to domestic violence, and about situations where a child had witnessed violence from loan sharks due to their parents' money situation. As part of their overall concern and close relationships with parents (which we focus on in the next chapter), schools were keen to alleviate any financial difficulty.

There were very practical considerations to providing food, even when participants were aware that the lack of food might not be pressing; they saw the food provided as meaning 'they could pay their electricity bill that month' (Bethany, Dimbleby Nursery). Genevieve at Webb Primary School explained that their motto was 'take this and save the money for that' because families could not have food *and* pay bills. Providing food removed part of one major cost for families, and freed up money for other things. As we will see, however, some of the participants' comments were less sympathetic about parents' financial situations and their choices as parents.

Deficit discourses about families

Among the many thoughtful and kind comments made by participants about food bank provision, we also identified a number of deficit discourses about families relating to parenting, budgeting and food choices. At times, our data reflect the production of individualised neoliberal subjectivities, where the parents who use the food bank are seen as individually responsible for their own situation, and are constructed as either deserving or undeserving of support. In these moments, we see how the research on public food banks is relevant to schools; many comments reflect wider societal 'regimes of truth' about less affluent people making poor decisions about where they spend their money, as seen among food bank volunteers in Garthwaite's ethnographic study (2016a). Some examples include:

> We also wanted to make it as healthy a food parcel as possible, we know that if we gave some of our families the money that they wouldn't necessarily spend that wisely. (Michael, Booth Primary School)

> We're not angels and our families make us cross sometimes, and they don't make very good decisions sometimes. So, yes, they can come to the food stall, and you know that they've spent money in a place that you personally wouldn't prioritise it, but then we've not lived their life in their shoes that makes them make those decisions. I can't put my value system onto them, and I'm sort of OK with that. It doesn't mean we don't get frustrated and things. (Charlotte, Lansbury Primary School)

As we see in Charlotte's comments, these discourses were sometimes deployed alongside sympathetic comments, such as this participant who voiced her shock at 'how little they have':

> I go out on home visits when the children start, and going into the homes of some of the people. It's just – it takes you by surprise because of how little they have. So it's – and I remember a few years ago going on one home visit, and I asked them what's their favourite toys, what do they enjoy playing with. And the parents said that they don't have no toys. All they've got is the phone, so they just sit there on the phone. Which impacts massively on their development and their learning. (Natalie, Rashford Nursery School)

At the same time as expressing surprise and (implicitly) sympathy about the lack of toys, Natalie also suggests a failure on the part of the parents to realise that only playing with a phone is not going to help children's development.

The most common negative points were related to food choices, particularly among the staff in early years settings: fruit and vegetables were described as 'not something they would necessarily get at home' (Audrey, Field Nursery School), and Naomi at Rashford Nursery School explained, 'they're not getting a lot of good nutrients'. Helen at Brown Pre-School commented, 'they're not accessing the right nutrition', noting how parents gave children bags of sweets at pick-up time. These comments reflect popular discourses of 'good' child nutrition, including eating 'five a day' (fruit and vegetables) and the relationship with being 'ready to learn'. They suggest children need to be not only fed, but fed with healthy food in order to learn and enjoy their time at the nursery. Helen is critical of what parents give their children, and made several comments to this effect. Here, she commented on the impact of food on children's behaviour, saying some were 'permanently hungry' and had 'extremely poor diets', so they give the family food, because 'when parents get the money it's initially straight into frozen pizzas, sweets, chocolates, crisps'. This results in parents unable to cope with their child who is 'climbing up the walls all the time' and asking the school for help, in her view. Thus, we see how food, parenting and behaviour are intertwined within this deficit discourse, which suggests parents are to some extent to blame for children being both hungry and 'climbing up the walls', with the result being an increase in workload. Similar links between diet and hyperactivity were made at some schools; for example, Sasha at Twining Primary School described problems with sleep and food as related to E numbers, and commented that when a parent raised concerns about ADHD, she thought 'you need to look at the diet'. While Sasha did caveat this comment with, 'But that's just a one-off child. The rest of the children, they *are* hungry', the link made quite casually between diet and behaviour suggests a well-established discourse. She later stated, 'if you're eating the wrong foods that are heavy in carbohydrates, you're sleepy all the time. So we find our kids have trouble getting out of bed in the morning and it's all just linked, isn't it?' Thus, food choices were linked with other school issues such as punctuality and attendance quite easily.

Returning to Helen, although she was critical of parents' choices, she also recognised that these choices were shaped by the environment too:

> To Tesco's, so it's like a mile down the road. Like I say most of our families if they're coming to do a shop they would jump in a taxi, either walk down or get the bus down … From their perspective you can go to the local shop and get a frozen pizza for £1, or you can get a microwave meal, or there's a chip shop and there's a kebab house that does burgers and pizzas, relatively cheap food. So, I had a researcher come to me from – they were commissioned by the local council to find out about access to healthy food. They were asking why are people not eating healthy. I said, 'Because it's not on their doorstep. It's not available to them.' (Helen, Brown Pre-School)

Helen's comments echo the findings of studies which suggest the problem of 'food deserts' in urban areas (Smith & Thompson, 2022), although her pre-school is in a rural area. The local supermarket which sells cheaper food is a mile away, which is a long way to walk with a pushchair and heavy bags, and a taxi would incur an additional cost (and many families do not have cars, she implies). Local public transport options are limited. Thus, families rely on the local shop which does not sell healthy food, but is cheap. Helen's comments reflect the problems of the local food environment, alongside disapproval of food choices, suggesting a vicious circle which ultimately disadvantages the local children. While these quotes reflect a wider debate about the food system of the UK, which is often politicised (Edwards, 2023), they also indicate a way in which food is another way to construct poorer families as responsible for their own problems, which in turn the schools feel responsible for solving. Helen also commented that not only was there no healthy food around, but also parents lacked 'the education ... to understand the benefits, because you've got people with – there's a lot of domestic abuse, drug issues, alcohol issues; eating healthy is not at the forefront of their mind'. She also mentioned that when she talked to parents about healthy eating, 'it falls on deaf ears', meaning parents do not listen. Helen combines an understanding of the problems of the food environment with a deficit discourse about parents' lack of education on the benefits of food; for her, at least some of the fault of children's poor nutrition lies with the parents.

Participants based in the schools' kitchens were also keen to talk about the need for parents to make good food choices, sometimes assuming a lack of investment in children's future 'relationship with food', as we see here with Greg, an apprentice chef:

> There will be children that won't be having a nutritious diet outside of the nursery. And I think to develop a healthy relationship with food, you have to do it early on, to be familiar with vegetables and how they taste and acclimatised to them so that you're not reliant on a microwave meal that's just full of salt and sugar to give you that kind of hit. You've got to start it young otherwise you set yourself up for trouble later on down the line. (Greg, Wilson Nursery)

Again, in these comments, the nursery is positioned as compensating for parents' inadequacies in terms of choosing food; educating children about vegetables so that they are not 'reliant' on high-sugar and high-salt foods. This is a long-term investment in children's future health, in this construction. Greg also talked about how when they get a 'good delivery' he can leave out food for families that they normally 'wouldn't be comfortable buying in the supermarket because they're not quite sure how to prepare it', and offered parents advice on cooking unfamiliar food. This assumes it is a lack of knowledge or willingness that prevents parents from taking some foods, rather than a matter of choice or taste.

At Booth Primary School, Michelle (the chef) commented on parents' choice not to provide breakfast; she explained that some children say '"I don't do breakfast," and "I haven't got time, I got up late, my mum doesn't do breakfast. My dad doesn't do breakfast"', but she thought, 'well that's not coming from you'. It is not clear whether parents do not provide breakfast because of lack of food or due to lack of time, but in Michelle's view this choice is being transferred onto children, who would naturally want breakfast. Michelle also commented on parents' choices about access to snacks, contrasting them with her own mother, who 'was very strict on what we ate as children' and when:

> I get a sense that children are more free to just go and take stuff out of the cupboard which means there's no control. If you've got two, three, four, five or six children and everyone is grabbing stuff out of the cupboard there's – where's the control? … it's up to you as a parent to say 'no, you have siblings, we all need to eat, so you can't do that'. One child said, 'My mum has put a lock on it' and I thought well OK, fair enough. That shouldn't be necessary.

This comment was related to the food bank in that Michelle explained that parents needed to 'top up' at the food banks because 'everything will go in a day if you allow it'; thus, the need for the food bank was linked to parents failing to take control of what children eat, particularly in larger families.

There is also an implied problem with discipline, if a lock is the only way to prevent children from taking food from the cupboard.

Similar disapproving comments were made in relation to the food that parents at the primary school food banks chose to take home. In one interview, Grace and Genevieve at Webb Primary School were talking about popular items such as ready meals (because they are low cost to heat up) and 'biscuits, cakes' (Grace), and contrasting this with 'the vegetables, like it's really sad but they're the last thing to go' (Genevieve). Here, we see the complexity of the poor choices narrative playing out in relation to the food bank at Webb Primary School; as school leaders Grace and Genevieve are happy to provide food for families in need, but they are also 'sad' that parents do not choose vegetables. This may be because of the additional cost of cooking vegetables, but there is still disapproval of the choice of parents to take biscuits and cakes; they went on to comment on the lack of nutrition that results. This echoes the discussion on choice of food (Garthwaite, 2016a), where choice becomes a luxury for the affluent while the poor should eat what they are given. The choice to have biscuits and cakes is constructed as problematic for children's nutrition, although many more affluent families would eat such 'treats' regularly. Genevieve's solution to the issue is to step in, however, providing nutritious food at lunchtime, and thus alleviate the problem. Again, the parents are constructed as failing, sometimes through their environment, but the school is seen as solving this problem.

A further point of criticism, related to food, was the choices parents made about how children spend their time out of school. For example, the practices of both putting children to bed early and keeping children out late were mentioned by early years staff, who were unsure 'whether that's because they don't have the food or whether it's convenient for them' (Gita, Wilson Nursery). This lack of routine was seen as meaning 'they're maybe not as settled as they would like them to be' (Bethany, Dimbleby Nursery). Thus, sympathy with parents' food insecurity was combined with disapproval of parenting practices (especially as sleep is seen as vital at this age). As Tarkiainen (2022) comments, 'people can apply flexible and even contradictory everyday moral reasoning when talking about who deserves help or wealth and why' (p 104).

The pervasiveness of the deserving/undeserving poor trope (Garthwaite, 2017; Tarkiainen, 2022) was apparent in the many mentions of families who 'took advantage' of the food bank. These comments suggest that school staff felt they were able to assess who deserved free food, and who did not. While we did not ask about this, comments such as these arose in participants' responses, particularly to the question of disadvantages of having a food bank. Michelle at Booth Primary School mentioned 'people who don't actually need to top up, but just want to come and get some free food', while Helen at Brown Pre-School commented on 'parents that owe some money to the nursery saying that they're really struggling but yet they've just booked a holiday'. Naomi at Rashford Nursery School said, 'You do get the odd parent that takes advantage. So you do have to know our families'; she explained that she sometimes offered help with money matters, but 'then they don't want to know', leaving her doubting whether they were really in need. She concluded, 'You do have to have – be a little bit cynical sometimes and not be a soft touch with some of the families and some of the cultures that are represented in our make-up of our families.'

Although some respondents have particular views of parents which made them more likely to see them as 'taking advantage', Naomi's comments also suggest a deficit discourse of undeservingness. She offers financial advice to parents and when this is refused, she views the parents as not really needing help or the free food, and so the school needs to avoid being a 'soft touch'. School staff have to 'know our families' and their 'cultures', and be cynical, or unfairness will result.

At Twining Primary School, Sasha was less sure about parents taking advantage of the food bank, saying there were 'one off' issues with children coming in with new trainers despite the parent using the food bank. What was clear from this comment and the following one from Bethany at Dimbleby Nursery was that school leaders need to consider the issue of parents taking advantage within their decisions on the food bank:

> A question I get asked quite a lot is, 'How do you know people aren't just taking advantage of the food bank?' but actually, I genuinely believe that none of our families here are. They're very grateful. Some might take extra, but it will be because they're helping Nan or they're helping their next door neighbour, but definitely.

Bethany has a more sympathetic viewpoint, that families taking more might be helping others, but the fact that this question is frequently asked suggests a wider concern with fairness in relation to the free food, which builds on the longstanding discourses of who deserves help discussed previously.

These deficit discourses matter because they show how, even though many staff are working very hard to address the problem of child poverty, this work can sit alongside deficit discourses about families. Helping families does not necessarily mean that staff approve of these parents, or their choices. These statements are what Tarkiainen (2022) refers to as a continuous performance of the discourse of deservingness, rhetorically positioning some families as failing to make the most of what they are offered in terms of free food. We see how the discourse of the un/deserving poor remains, with some families seen as deserving of help more than others, if they make more sensible choices. Alongside this, there is the need for schools to alleviate the problems caused by parents' bad choices for children where they can, so that schools become responsible for not only feeding families, but also dealing with the wider problems of behaviour or poor nutrition caused by parents' choices.

Impact on particular groups of families

A final aspect of the impact on families was the specific effects of having a food bank on families who faced additional problems. Housing was a major issue mentioned by participants, which was clearly related to parents' ability to cook and store food and thus significant in terms of food bank provision. Several families were mentioned as being in temporary accommodation, including hotels, with no way to cook food. Natalie at Rashford Nursery School explained that a family living in a hotel had no cooking facilities:

> Mum was really upset when she was coming to drop the children off, because she can't give them breakfast, she can't give them lunch. So she was having to buy takeaways and that. So that was affecting what little money she did have. So we made a food parcel up for her, which was – had a lot of stuff that just needed hot water: Pot Noodles, the porridge that you can make with water, because she had access to a kettle in her room. So we sent her those, which really, really helped her.

This family were placed in a position where their financial situation was exacerbated by having to buy expensive food due to the lack of cooking facilities in the hotel, but the school provided particular food which 'really, really helped her'. This shows how relationships facilitate better provision, and how important it is for schools to understand what parents need and respond to this. Similar situations occurred in other settings, such as at Dimbleby Nursery, where Bethany noted a family were unable to use the 'tins and rice' from the foodbank as they had no oven or hob. At Brown Pre-School, Helen noted that they could not assume parents will have 'the right cooking utensils' or 'pots and pans'. Schools are required to be responsive in their responsibility to feed families, and otherwise care for their needs. Similarly, at Lansbury Primary School, the headteacher was providing a range of support to a family who were evicted and placed in a hotel temporarily:

> They're in a Travelodge somewhere, miles away from school ... in a Travelodge, so that you have no cooking facilities and no washing facilities. So it's not because necessarily they don't have the money for food ... then again, they're not even really allowed a microwave in their rooms in these hotels. So they have takeaways every night, because that's all that's open to them. It is absolutely horrific. (Andrea, Lansbury Primary School)

The school was providing bus passes to this family to allow them to travel to school and extra nursery hours for the younger child. They were also planning to provide facilities for families to wash and dry their clothes on site, but there was also acute awareness of the particular needs of these families in relation to food, as the hotel limited the parents' options. Grace at Webb Primary School mentioned a family in a similar situation, 'having meal deals for their dinner', which she disapproved of until they told her, 'We don't need to heat that up.' She noted that 'there's families with no electricity and there's families with no running water'. Stephanie at Oliver Children's Centre discussed the needs of sanctuary seekers in particular:

> We work with, for example, lots of sanctuary seekers who are living in hotel accommodation. They are catered for, but they're not necessarily able to – it might be that their dietary requirements and so on aren't catered for. So accessing a pantry is ideal for them, but they wouldn't fit the criteria of going to a food bank because they don't have permanent residence. So situations like that and various other things that maybe somebody is sofa-surfing at the moment and they haven't got an address and so on. So they're not able to access

food banks. So we set up our food pantry model with that in mind, that we don't have an eligibility criteria, anybody can come along and we don't tell you whether or not you need it or not.

For some families, the choices they are making related to food are significantly affected by circumstance, whether that be temporary accommodation or not having access to electricity or water (perhaps due to not paying bills). For Stephanie, the model of a food pantry where you can choose your food without needing a referral allows the most vulnerable people to access food. Those families without recourse to public funds were seen as particularly in need of support from food banks; Abigail at Field Nursery School noted that not being able to work means 'they're really stuck': 'That's what I hear from families in that situation they're just stuck because they actually quite want to work and they want to do as much as they can do to be part of the community for their child. So those families particularly use the resource of the food.' These families, who are unable to access benefits due to their temporary immigration status, are unable to increase their income by working either. Abigail is sympathetic to this situation, and how the families are prevented from helping themselves. In these cases, parents are seen as victims of their situations, and the school has to adapt what it can offer in response. This contrasts with some of the previous comments, where parents were seen as failing to help themselves, and returns us to the discourse of un/deservingness.

Conclusion

This chapter has used the voices of the school staff to illustrate the impact of having a food bank on children's learning and then on families. We explored how biological and neurological discourses of hunger and cognitive effects are used to emphasise the importance of food for children, and the interesting lack of perceived impact on physical activity. We argued that the impact on children's wellbeing was more significant, however; it is not simply about not being hungry, but also not worrying about being hungry, or your parents being hungry. Food banks also allowed children to participate in ordinary childhood activities with dignity, and this was seen as key; as this area is largely unexplored in the literature, this is an important contribution to the field. We argue that food banks are part of a school's practices of inclusion because they allow all children to participate in school life.

We then examined the impact on family wellbeing, and the complexity of how staff discuss families and their needs. While many are positive, there were numerous times when participants deployed deficit discourses which positioned the parents as making bad choices relating to food, as poor parents in general, or (though rarely) as 'taking advantage'. We also argued that a contrasting discourse was used for particularly vulnerable families in temporary accommodation. These different positions suggest the continued operation of the un/deserving poor binary, with all families being helped, but some viewed as being more deserving.

What we can conclude, overall, is that each school is serving a different community with different needs, and the food banks have a positive impact on both the child and the wider family. The school is ideally placed to understand and cater for the needs of their families, as we will see in more detail in the following chapter, making them an ideal hub for welfare support. Teachers know who needs shoes so they can run around, or who needs to be given food they can use without cooking. At the same time, some are negative about parents and their choices, further complicating this responsibility of the school to deal with hunger.

While we acknowledge the limitation of this research in exploring the impact on families, in that we do not hear from the parents who use the food bank (discussed in Chapter One), we would also argue that the views of the staff are important in understanding the full range of impacts on children and their families. They see the impact in their everyday lives, and are able to assess the impact on learning and participation. In the following chapter, we move on to discussing why the schools choose to operate food banks.

FIVE

Why do schools have food banks?

Introduction

Why do schools offer food banks? Is it because children are hungry, because they need saving from parents who make bad choices, or because the only way to get children to learn is to feed them first? And what's in it for the schools? Is it about improving results, or improving behaviour, or about a moral sense of obligation to families with longstanding relationships with the school? The answer is that schools have food banks for all these reasons, to a varying degree; as we have seen, they are committed to helping families, but they are also sometimes disapproving of parents. Food banks help children to learn, but they also help families more widely. In this chapter, we explore in more depth the advantages for schools of having a food bank, and then the deeper moral justifications. The aim here is not to explore the reasons why families are faced with food insecurity, as this has been explored elsewhere (Daly & Kelly, 2015; Treanor, 2020), but instead to consider why schools offer this provision given the circumstances families find themselves in.

This chapter explores how leaders balance the advantages of operating a food bank with the additional costs, beginning with a discussion of the impact on home–school relationships, including the mutually beneficial outcome of increasing the information schools have about families' difficulties, and in turn their willingness to come to school for help. We examine how the operation of the food bank shifts the subjectivities of teacher and parent, with complex power dynamics in operation. We consider how difficulties can arise in relationships and the challenges schools face in dealing with issues of eligibility for free food without a formal framework. Overall, we argue, however, that the schools benefit from the food bank in multiple ways due to the closer relationships with parents.

Beyond this, we argue that the justification for committing time and energy to the food bank arises from the impact on children and families discussed in Chapter Four, but also from moral and practical reasonings. Teachers feel they need to provide food when faced with children who are hungry, and to compensate for the impact of poverty on children in their care. Schools offer a practical solution, in that parents attend the site regularly and there is reduced stigma. School leaders are also pragmatic about their unique position as the service which sees children regularly, arguing that if they did not provide food, no one would. This section examines the ambiguity of feeling about stepping beyond education into welfare-related work, and the complexities of decision-making around what can and should be done by schools. This leads into the broader debate we examine in Chapter Six on how schools have become responsibilised to compensate for the inadequacies of the welfare state.

Home–school relationships

A major benefit of the schools operating food banks was the improvement in home–school relationships which resulted. However, this was not only a benefit, but also a cause, as schools with their close relationships with parents felt responsible for these families, and thus motivated to help. Here, two headteachers, Andrea and Charlotte, explain:

> Primary schools are so different to secondary. We see parents every day. They come and collect their kids. We go, 'Hi, how are you?' – an informal chat. Which means they can go, 'Miss, can I just have a word with you? I'm really struggling with ...' or, 'Any spare uniform anywhere? Because I just can't afford ...' Those opportunities for informal chats which lead to us understanding the issues far better, seeking ways to help. That is a very unique position for primary schools to be in. (Andrea, Lansbury Primary School)

> We just know the families really well. We know what's going on in – not everything, but we know a lot of what's going on in their lives. They tend to talk to us not just about when they need food. We're there when they're experiencing other difficulties. We're all on the gates every single morning, and every single afternoon. So it's just a very – we're just familiar faces to them. (Charlotte, Rowntree Primary School)

This opportunity to talk directly to parents on a daily basis meant that primary school teachers were more keenly aware of the issues facing families, and relationships are established in ways which foster communication. While public food banks might offer 'meaningful encounters between people of different social positions' (Cloke et al, 2017, p 708), school food banks can be seen as providing meaningful encounters between people positioned differently in relation to the school, as well as perhaps of different social standing. These relationships were not always simple, as we will discuss, but the closeness of families to the school environment in both physical and emotional terms was a key component in all the schools in how and why the food bank operated.

Awareness of needs

Schools had a good understanding of the issues faced by their families, and thus were able to support families better, as Bethany at Dimbleby Nursery explained:

> It opens up that conversation with the parents. It just means that we're more easily able to help in certain situations ... if the children mention something that they haven't got, you can just maybe put a bag on their peg or just offer it to the parents when they come, depending on the parent and how open they are to that. It means that it's opened up other avenues for us, like I say, like the clothes bank and the hygiene bank and other ways that we can help. The more communication we have with the parent about those sort of situations, the best we can tailor our provision and the help that we offer and what we do for the children. Obviously, the more we know about their background and home life, the more we know how to support them in nursery.

Thus, for Bethany, the knowledge gained allows them to be more helpful to families – as noted by Andrea, this is a the 'unique position' of primary schools and nurseries and their relationships with parents who are usually present at the setting twice a day. This knowledge is also helpful in tailoring help such as through additional organisations, and in supporting the child themselves in the nursery.

Often, the organiser of the food bank was also someone who understood the particularities of the challenges local families faced. In some cases, a key person was the 'expert' in the local families, such as at Twining Primary School, where Sarah, as a local resident who had worked in the school for decades, had an incredibly detailed knowledge of the families' needs: 'Sometimes I'll know which family is needing what, so it will go straight to that family. Otherwise, it's just a generic thing. The same with household goods. Families will say to me, 'Sarah, if you get any rugs, can you put them on one side for me?' It's those little things really.' Sarah explained that she knew when a family moved into a particular row of houses that they'd need rugs as there were hard floors; this was the level of detail with which she operated. This meant provision could be tailored to each family, for example by providing nappies for a family expecting a new baby, or as we saw in Chapter Four, food that didn't need to be heated for a family with no cooking facilities. A similar attention to detail was apparent at Dimbleby Nursery, where they collected information to help distribute clothes from a charity:

> So some are new, some are second-hand, but they're all donations, but they offer children and adults. So when we send off for the – we have to do a spreadsheet. So for each family, we put who's in the family, how old they are, what size nappies they are, what size shoes they are, so for everybody. (Bethany, Dimbleby Nursery)

Bethany acknowledged that collecting this information was time-consuming, but noted that it was necessary to make the most of the donated clothes and ensure everyone got something useful. Provision could be made efficient and effective, based on the expertise of staff. At this nursery, the key person was Brenda, who lived locally and had a clear sense of how the food bank benefitted local families:

> So because I know a lot of families outside the nursery, I know how they are really struggling. So when the food bank came in, trust me, it was amazing. They see me on the street and their faces and the way they are appreciating what we've been doing, some of them will come up to me, especially during the weekends and the holidays … So they have the chance to have a chit-chat with me and they tell me how the food bank has been really helping them. (Brenda, Dimbleby Nursery)

Several food banks were reliant on a key person, and that person became an expert in the families and what was needed. While this meant provision was precarious, it also meant that families could build those relationships with one key person, adding to the sense of trust. As Audrey at Field Nursery School explained, this meant she could also direct families to other useful services; similarly, Stella, a volunteer at the food bank at Oliver Children's Centre, could help families, including those who spoke the same community language:

> I'm probably the first person that they will speak to and then usually if it's something I can signpost them to, like, because we work with the children's centres and stuff like that if it's something we can't help them with we will signpost them. (Audrey)

> When they don't know anything, I can explain them. I can help them to have that, have registration for something or I can indicate to them for someone if they need an appointment or interpret or children, helping for speech and language. (Stella)

Having these relationships with staff with knowledge of the community benefitted parents, while in turn the schools benefitted from being able to gather information on families' needs. These 'meaningful encounters' (Cloke et al, 2017) led, as we discuss next, to improvements in connections and trust.

Improved connections and trust

It has long been established that positive school–parent relationships have the potential to contribute to children's learning outcomes, primarily through improving children's motivation and attitude towards school and learning (Bishop, 2023; Desforges & Abouchaar, 2003). Participants reported that having a food bank had improved relationships with parents, particularly in terms of making connections and building trust. Catherine at Rowntree Primary School noted, 'I feel like our relationships are much stronger with our community.' This was helped by the addition of other services, such as translating forms or helping with IT issues, which could be shared with parents during the time the food bank was operating.

> I think the parents see the school as a safe haven, in a sense, now that we're seen as people that care, people beyond just educators, I think that's broken down quite a lot of barriers with our families. So they will come to us now and share their needs with us and share their financial situation and maybe they wouldn't have done beforehand. (Michael, Booth Primary School)

> Sarah [staff member] built up a relationship with families over the years and they really trust her and they will go to her with everything. Even if they've got immigration issues. We've had a couple of parents who have been trafficked into the country. They're very open and honest with her. (Sasha, Twining Primary School)

In these cases, the close relationships allowed the school to help the parents more, by signposting help with financial problems or with immigration issues. The parents in Twining Primary School had disclosed that they were in the country illegally at the food bank, as they had been trafficked into the UK. Another parent had shared that her partner was awaiting a trial for murdering a family member, which had resulted in her son struggling with behaviour at school. As the head Sasha noted, 'we wouldn't have known that if Sarah didn't have those relationships with the parents'.

These honest relationships were enabled by the regularity of attending the food bank and the careful work of the staff in building a culture of trust. Often, this trusting relationship was talked about as a slowly developing one, which could be speeded up by the time spent at the food bank:

> They kind of know that actually, we don't judge them once they get to know us. But you've got to build that relationship first. (Naomi, Rashford Nursery School)

> I think in some cases, it has definitely helped in that they, one, I think open up to you a little bit more. It helps us as a nursery to know about the family situation which then that conversation leads onto other things, which are obviously important for us to know about the children and the background. Also, we then have parents who once you get over that hurdle of them being open about that and speaking about that, then they'll speak to you about other things that they need help with as well, that maybe they wouldn't have felt like they could before. (Bethany, Dimbleby Nursery)

Getting over the 'hurdle' of establishing trust was one of the benefits of the food bank, as sharing food as a universal human point of connection appeared to help build relationships. Sarah at Twining Primary School talked about parents trying on some of the clothes and laughing, making connections with staff and other parents even when they could not speak English. Making the food bank a sociable and relaxed place also seemed to be key. Matt, the food bank volunteer at Booth Primary School, explained how the food bank affected relations:

> I think it's a bonding thing isn't it. It's a provision, you bond with those who provide don't you? I mean I don't even work for the school, but I know that I have a relationship with the members of the food store, and they don't know me but they like the idea of me as an individual because I provide them with food.

This unique context of the food store, as it was called at Booth Primary School, allowed Matt as an outsider to bond with families. Similarly, at Wilson Nursery, Gabrielle talked about the importance of interactions when parents were accessing the free food:

> When we do have those interactions when there are parents coming in to have a look, we can have those conversations and you know that's an important moment for us because we can get to know them a bit more. And, you never know, if they are struggling, they could disclose to us, you know, 'It's been a really difficult week', or a really difficult month and you can then build those deeper connections with them. And sometimes it is good just to have that chit-chat, we don't get a lot of time in the nursery to have a quick conversation with parents … sometimes, you know, you get those two, two to five minutes to just have a chat and talk about anything. It could be the child development, it could be their day, it could be any stresses they have. It could be a joke to make them laugh. So it is imperative to our relationship that we have with our parents.

Thus, the food provision was the location for the everyday interactions – the chit-chat and jokes – that are the foundation for building relationships. There was also kindness within these interactions, as Andrea at Lansbury Primary School explained:

> Families feel supported. They are meeting kind people who say, 'Yeah, of course, go and have a look. Take what you want. A bit of extra food here, a bit of extra food there' … So if you know we care enough to get you some food and there's some clothes and there's some pots and pans and there's some toys and do, 'Hello, help yourself', it's, we're trying to remove the 'us and them' barrier and othering.

As mentioned by Garthwaite (2016a) in her study of public food banks, having somewhere to go with kind people to talk to made a difference to these families, who were being treated with respect and compassion. It also helps to break down the barriers between home and school, the feeling of 'us and them'. There were also social benefits for more isolated parents; Sophie at Twining Primary School commented, 'They feel included. They have somebody they can talk to.' She continued, 'You see them coming out of the food bank and they genuinely look happier, because there's food in the cupboard.'

In other schools, the food banks were also seen as important as indications that schools and parents were working together. For both parents and children, this was seen as a key message – that the school was 'on their side'. This led to more trust, and in turn to a more open and supportive relationship being built:

> I think the biggest impact on the children's wellbeing is the feeling that they get from their mum and dad that school are helping them … school and home are on the same side. (Grace, Webb Primary School)

> I think having the food bank there it is like saying we're here, we support you. (Martha, Booth Primary School)

> I definitely think the relationships between us and families has been stronger because of it. I think they know that we are there to support them and to help them. (Catherine, Rowntree Primary School)

These comments suggest a sense of shared mission, that parents and school were working together to help the child as much as possible. At the early years settings, similar comments were made about trust:

> I think the parents trust us more, and have a better relationship with us. Obviously, that in turn helps the

children with their bonds with us, and they get to know us better when they're here with us. (Helen, Brown Pre-School)

I think some – I think once they do open up to us, then they're not embarrassed. And it does make it [the relationship] a lot stronger because they feel that they can come and speak to us about anything. (Natalie, Rashford Nursery School)

These improved relationships allowed the school to help more, and to understand the child better, because the parents were able to explain their situations. As Andrea argued, 'without communication and relationships, we have nothing'.

Difficulties in relationships

While the overall conclusion of most participants was that the food bank was beneficial in terms of relationships, there were some instances of the food bank causing tensions with parents or between parents. This reminds us of the sometimes ambivalent viewpoints of staff towards parents accessing the food bank, discussed in Chapter Four. As well as the perceived problem of parents 'taking advantage' mentioned by some participants, there were examples of the food bank itself being a source of division, such as at Lansbury Primary where there were some parents who questioned how the school decided who to support. The headteacher Andrea commented it was a 'balancing act between keeping people's dignity and helping and trying to avoid, "Well, how come you paid for her to go on the trip, but you didn't pay for my kids to go on the trip?"'. Andrea explained how the school has to keep some of its provision 'low key', in order to avoid parents questioning why some families receive help and others don't, and the tensions between different community groups in terms of who was receiving support: she explained, 'Sometimes people go, "How come the Romanian families are getting this food? You're favouring the Romanians.'" In a situation where there are no rules for eligibility, the decision to help some families is entirely up to the headteacher, as Andrea went on to explain: 'I've heard other headteachers getting it really in the neck, going, 'How come you helped that family? You didn't help me. You always help them.' So then that thing of trying to monitor who's had what. That's not our job.'

This role as arbiter of who deserves help is an additional burden on the head, and one which can be difficult to justify to parents who may not see the whole context, and are not privy to all the information for confidentiality reasons. Andrea also explained that families complained about grants that the school had no control over, thinking they made the decision; she concluded that 'it's so fraught'. Thus, in this case, the food bank and other provisions further complicated parent–school relationships more widely, and caused tensions between different groups of parents, as well as strengthening the relationship with those families in need.

There were also mentions of parents who complained about what was on offer at the food bank, leading to suggestions of a lack of gratitude from the staff:

> We have five pantries around. So sometimes, they know the two or three pantry and then they come here and say, 'All right, because why the pantry, for example, give to me this, this and this and this. Here, you don't give' ... They are not satisfied with half of things ... it's not only you have a nice family, nice mum and dad is coming, but having someone who's like, 'I don't like this, I don't like that', and then they buy the fruit and vegetable, they don't have enough because they don't like this, don't like that. (Stella, Oliver Children's Centre)

> We are not getting a lot of funding for the food bank. So sometimes, they [parents] do say that, 'Why is it that

these days, you guys don't offer a lot of things, a wide range of things?' Like, let's say, for the toilet tissue. It used to be four in a pack or six in a pack, but now because we are hard of money, we do take them out and then we single them. So sometimes, they are not really happy about that. (Brenda, Dimbleby Nursery)

Stella explains how families compare what is on offer at the different food pantries at children's centres (where families pay a reduced amount for a set amount of food), and complain that she doesn't have everything they like. These problematic customers are compared with the 'nice mums and dads' who attend. Brenda explains similarly that parents complain about the range of goods on offer and how they are given out, including having single toilet rolls there due to lack of funding. These comments suggest a tension between wanting to help families and adapting to their needs and desires, and the practical realities of what is on offer. This links to the discussion in the food banks literature about respecting food bank users' preferences, and Garthwaite's (2017) argument that being able to choose what you eat should not be a luxury from which the poor are excluded. Indeed, Brenda continued, 'Although they don't have the money, but they still like quality things, and you can't blame them.' She understands that people need to be afforded the dignity of choice, but she is also limited by the financial situation of the school from giving out whole packs of toilet roll. These parents make her job harder, and the tough decisions faced by staff running the food banks can in turn create tensions with parents.

There were also some difficult relationships with families caused by a perceived lack of gratitude at Brown Pre-School, where Helen, as previously mentioned, used some deficit discourses about parents in general. In this case, the problem of being ungrateful was also related to the problem of 'dependency'. She gave an example of complaints about the food at other food banks, and then noted:

> We've provided a food parcel to a gentleman at our other site, and my husband was walking the dog, walking the same way and he took a couple of things out of the bag and threw the rest in the bin. We've become disheartened sometimes and we feel like yes, giving people a foodbank parcel isn't the best way, but like I say there's a concern that there becomes a dependency on it, so they think if I'm going to save £40 a week from them, then I have a spare £40. (Helen, Brown Pre-School)

Helen's comments here echo wider discourses of concern about dependency on benefits; she suggests people will see the free food as meaning they have 'a spare £40' rather than needing the food to feed their children. This is compounded by complaints about what is on offer and people throwing away some of the food, leaving Helen feeling 'disheartened', and questioning if the food banks are 'the best way'. Nonetheless, she remains committed to the provision, as we see in the rest of her interview, and determined to help the children at the pre-school.

In many cases, the food bank opened up a new element to the relationship between parent and school, which could be both a positive and a negative for staff. Overall, our data suggest that there are more positives than negatives in terms of relationships. Although there might sometimes be tensions, this improved relationship, which included a greater sense of trust and togetherness, was a major reason for operating a food bank.

Moral justifications

Participants offered a number of reasons why the food bank was beneficial and necessary during the interviews, in addition to the improved relationships discussed previously. For many, there was a moral sense of obligation towards children and families that they saw every day. As Grace (Webb Primary School) explained, the school supports families because 'we have to';

referring to children's hunger, she said, 'You can't not see it.' Staff explained about occasions where children were clearly hungry, and they responded; there seemed in these accounts to be no question about feeding children there and then if that was what was needed. For example, Brenda at Dimbleby Nursery commented, 'you can see that they feel a bit weak … you give it to them, they will sit down and they will eat it'. Others explained:

> If any child comes in and says they've not eaten, or if they come in and there's something not right, the staff will go, 'What did you have for breakfast today?' and then they're scooped and we feed them. (Charlotte, Rowntree Primary School)

> As little as they are, they were coming to school without eating. We've had the odd child faint and then teachers come down for an apple, or orange, or whatever I've got in here. (Michelle, Booth Primary School)

Moral obligations were a further clear motivation for helping families; faced with hungry children, the instinct of these professionals is to care and help. This is a human instinct, but also a part of their professional identity, as Sasha at Twining Primary School explained: 'It's like we're humans and our natural instinct is to care. That's why I came into this profession. It's a caring profession.' This argument was repeated among many participants, who combined their human desire to care with their professional caring identity as teachers or early years practitioners. This job to 'care for them', in Catherine's view, meant staff ended up doing the extra job of feeding children:

> We do it because there's a need, but it's not our job to feed the children in the community. Our job is to look after them and educate them and care for them while they're at school, not to feed them at the weekends or

holidays, but we can't help but be concerned about that.
(Catherine, Rowntree Primary School)

Catherine's comment hints at the tensions between the educational role and the welfare role, which we return to in more detail in the following chapter. But her comments also show how the provision is driven by a very human response of concern for children's wellbeing; as she says, 'We do it because there's a need'. Charlotte, at the same school, reiterated this viewpoint, suggesting a combination of moral responsibility and realism about what a hungry child could achieve: 'So we don't ever think, 'Why do I have to feed this child?' If that child's hungry, that child – could you concentrate on your work if you'd not eaten since your school dinner the day before? Of course you couldn't.'

These tensions between education and welfare played out differently in the early years settings, due to the less clear division between these purposes with younger children. There were similar comments made about caring for families being the justification for the food banks, but these feelings of care were complicated at Brown Pre-School, which was a privately run setting which needed to be profitable. Helen explained, in reference to other private settings which did not have food banks: 'if they're a business and they're wanting to be a profitable business there's no money in it for them. You're doing it from a moral obligation. You're doing it because your families need it.' This context of private provision makes the moral explanation even clearer: offering free food does not have any profit motive, but is instead motivated by the needs of families and a resulting 'moral obligation'.

At Booth Primary School, this moral purpose was linked with other factors in children's lives:

We know that we've definitely seen in recent months an increase in domestic violence, we've seen an increase in child protection issues and that we think is the result of pressures that is on families from not having enough funds. So we know that the more we can support those families in making sure they've got food then that pressure should ease and, therefore, there is the moral obligation to make sure that children are protected. (Michael, Booth Primary School)

For Michael, the food bank is part of alleviating the greater pressures on families, which might lead to additional problems such as domestic violence and child protection issues. Thus, for him, having a food bank is part of the school's moral obligation to protect children from harm, however indirectly this might work. Easing pressure on families through food is a straightforward route for the school to take, given the complexity of other issues families face.

An overriding argument was made in several interviews that schools *had to* offer food banks, because there was no one else to support families in food insecurity. The absence of alternatives meant that, morally, school staff felt they had to step in. When asked if she thought schools *should* have food banks, Lorraine at Peabody Primary School replied: 'It's really hard, isn't it? Probably not, but someone's got to do it, haven't they? Unfortunately, at the moment, we live in a time where they're needed and if we don't do it, who will?' Lorraine's objection here (the 'probably not') seems to lie in her rejection of a situation where food banks are needed, rather than to the schools running them. In this context, she argues that they have to do it because there is no one else to step in. This 'someone's got to do it' justification is, we would argue, built on the experiences of staff seeing hungry children, their awareness of the wider family pressures, and the overriding importance of caring for the children, all of which were identified earlier. The problem cannot be left unsolved, and so the school solves it. They are made responsible by this confluence of poverty, and their proximity to it, and the practicalities which mean that schools *can* operate food banks, which we will return to.

Practical justifications

As we have seen, there is a range of reasons why schools have food banks, many of which overlap; here, we consider the practical justifications. Our data suggest that schools are places where support can easily be accessed in terms of location, and are less daunting than a public food bank. Thus, they provide an ideal location for families to access the help they need in practical terms, but also have social benefits, as the school-based food bank is less stigmatising than a public food bank. The practical therefore mixes with the social and emotional reasoning in participants' explanations.

Ease of access

A key practical consideration related to the advantages of having the food bank located at the school or nursery site; this was a reason given why the school offered a food bank, as opposed to somewhere else. School-based food banks are easy to access for parents who would often be there twice a day anyway:

> Lots of our families haven't got the capacity to go somewhere else. So, for example, if you don't have a car, public transport is very expensive for an adult. So here, they have to come here to pick up their child or collect their child. (Grace, Webb Primary School)

> I think the thing about having it here is that we know we have lots of families coming in and out daily and, you know, we're a 62-place nursery so that alone is a lot of families that we can help. And sometimes they may not have time from day-to-day things, they may not have time to go to the local community, you know, if they've finished a nine to five shift, they're tired, they want to go home. So it's nice that we can have it here and it's something that will help them out with helping

their day run smoothly and hope it's helping the child's day run smoothly as well. So I think that's what is very good about having it in the nursery because they can come and go as they please and pick something up on the way, it's not a hassle or an extra thing to do. (Gabrielle, Dimbleby Nursery)

Marianne at Booth Primary School similarly commented that the school food bank meant 'you haven't got to go out in an evening'. This issue of convenience for families was very important in the explanations of why the food banks were successful and well used: issues such as public transport, lack of time, and having to go out again in the evening after work were all resolved by having the food bank at the school. This meant more families could access the provision. There were also mentions of not having to produce a voucher to attend, and the difficult opening times of public food banks. At the children's centre, where parents attend less regularly, there were similar advantages in terms of practicality: 'It's convenient because I think for all the ones who work here, we live local, and then we have the little area for the kids to stay. If we go somewhere else, I don't know if they have space enough, so we bring our children' (Stella, Oliver Children's Centre).

Stella explains that the location of the food pantry and the space provided for children make this provision attractive. The issue of location is identified in the wider food banks literature as significant, as food bank users need to be able to easily access the service and get home with the food they are given. Nonetheless, the idea that people in need will only access free food if it is convenient is also controversial to some, in a similar way to the problem of food bank users being 'picky' about what they receive (Garthwaite, 2016a). This disapproval was not present in our data, however; instead, respondents were very sympathetic to the practical reasons why families might prefer a school-based food bank over a traditional public food bank. Bethany at Dimbleby Nursery noted that, in relation to visiting a public food bank, 'We've noticed an increase in a lot of things here that would make that harder', such as poor transport and lack of time; she concludes, 'it just becomes another task that they're having to do'. In this context, the convenience of being able to access food at the nursery means it is the only realistic option.

There were further comparisons between the ease of accessing the school food bank and the public food banks. Nicola at Rashford Nursery School noted parents 'find it quite embarrassing … other people might see them' at public food banks. Genevieve at Webb Primary School noted that many food banks are in churches, and 'we have Jewish people, we have Muslim people who might not want to step into a church'. In contrast, the school food bank was a comfortable place:

> It's parents mixing with other parents I think that feels OK to them. When they go to the food bank and there are people that don't feel like they're from their community, in a sense, I think that doesn't feel quite as safe. (Michael, Booth Primary School)

> They really feel very comfortable [here] because sometimes you don't even have what you want. You know that there's another food bank somewhere, but just walking into the place, just going to collect the food, sometimes some of them feel a bit embarrassed or they feel a bit shy. But all I care, you are bringing your child anyway. So you drop your child, you pick it up. (Brenda, Dimbleby Nursery)

We see how going to a public food bank was seen as embarrassing in a way that the school food bank was not. As we see later in this section, the lack of stigma at school was important to school staff. Thus, there were both pull factors of having the food bank at school, such as convenience, but also push factors which made the public food banks less attractive.

Stephanie, who was involved in the food pantry at Oliver Children's Centre, explained how even operating at schools as an outside agency was challenging, due to safeguarding procedures, and 'you had to be buzzed in by staff to be able to access the pantry'. This comment points to the problem of barriers, both physical and social. When they tried to run a food pantry in a school, Stephanie found additional challenges because children there were not with their parents. Even though the pantry does not require a voucher or strict eligibility criteria (what Stephanie refers to as a 'self-assess model'), just having to be 'buzzed in' through the security door to access the food pantry is a limiting factor in who attends. In contrast, the children's centre is an ideal site, Stephanie explained, because '[e]veryone's already familiar with the setting. They've got a relationship already built with the children centre staff'. She went on to say: 'I think it means that there's, yes, a comfort in attending somewhere that you already know. It's not that overwhelming feeling of – for a lot of people, going to a new place is anxiety-inducing enough' (Stephanie, Oliver Children's Centre). For vulnerable communities, such as those with which Stephanie works, going to a familiar place such as a children's centre is important. This comfort was explained as a key reason for the food bank by many participants, due to the reduced stigma associated with a school food bank, which is the focus of the next section.

Reducing stigma

As suggested by the wider research literature (Purdam et al, 2015; Garthwaite, 2016b), there is still a great deal of stigma associated with using a food bank, according to our participants. There were references to families not taking food 'out of shame' (Helen, Brown Pre-School), and at Wilson Nursery, Gita explained why she wanted to move her free food provision to a more relaxed space, having already moved it to an office which parents passed by, referring to 'the shame around taking it'. Staff were acutely aware of the need to think about the shame and stigma of needing free food. They saw parents as feeling embarrassed, ashamed or shy using food banks outside of school, as we have seen, but in contrast, the location of the food bank at a site they are visiting for other reasons meant there can be more privacy around accessing free food:

> Some of our families are very – they don't want to do that [go elsewhere], because they don't want to be seen that they're having to use a food bank. So they have to be desperate to ask us about food, the food needs. And then us having food on-site means if we even get a sense of, like, they're struggling, we literally put food in a bag and say, 'Look, take that home.' They don't have to make a big thing of it. They don't have to ask in front of a load of people. They don't have to go and queue outside the food bank. I think people in this area, they're very – it's quite a close-knit area and people know what other – each people are doing. And there is a massive stigma around not having enough food I think, yes. (Naomi, Rashford Nursery School)

> It's a totally different game for our parents and our community to go and actually, physically reach out to someone and hand someone something [voucher] to say 'I'm really struggling, I need help', whereas this food bank, you can just turn up and take whatever you need and that's what we operate on. It's that there's no shame, there's no judgement, you don't have to explain anything at all. You just let us know that you need support and we're there. (Lesley, Peabody Primary School)

> I think I used the word dignity earlier, but I think families going to a food bank, I think families sometimes would avoid that just because of the stigma that comes with it. But going into the school, as I say, it seems like a safe

place and there isn't the stigma with that and I think that that's quite appealing to our families. (Michael, Booth Primary School)

This ease of access, both in terms of location and not having to produce a voucher or be seen to ask for help in public, was a key advantage of the school food banks. The lack of shame and stigma associated with the food banks in school was vital in justifying their location, and in them being well used by parents.

Several settings had gone to great lengths to reduce the stigma associated with accessing food – for example, through their portrayal of the food as 'food waste' which needed eating to save the environment (discussed in Chapter Three). Others did not call it a food bank at all, or called it a food stall or food pantry:

> I think the thing that makes it work is that they're coming to the building, so it basically is a food bank but it's not portrayed in that way, and they [parents] don't see it that way. (Abigail, Field Nursery School)

> I think from having called it a food stall we've never had – or if we do have any stigma with it, it's quite quickly overcome. (Catherine, Rowntree Primary School)

As Abigail went on to explain, 'anything that feels less like charity and more like a gift they seem more responsive to'; the food bank operated far more effectively and could help more families if it was not labelled as such. Similarly, at Rowntree Primary School, Catherine argues that calling it a food stall meant that there were long queues of parents waiting to use it, such was the lack of stigma associated with it.

In other cases, as discussed in Chapter Three, the food bank was located in a place and operated in a way that other families would not see who was using it. At Dimbleby Nursery, the food bank was at the entrance, because 'they wouldn't do it if they had to come in and ask' (Bethany); Brenda commented, 'Nobody even sees it.' At Wilson Nursery, it was in a private room 'so they [parents] would have to feel nothing going and taking something' (Gabrielle), and their chef commented, 'I would never want a parent to feel like they can't walk in to our pantry room because they don't want to be seen by other parents or staff to be in there.' At Twining Primary School, they deliberately located the food bank in a space where no teachers could see who was accessing it either, so that there was no sense that a child would be labelled by their parents being seen attending, as discussed in Chapter Three. This 'confidentiality' does not risk damaging the relationship built up with parents. Sasha judges that putting the food out on tables, as done at some schools, would not work with their parents, who are 'quite proud'. Sophie, a teacher at the school, also explained, 'We just try and be mindful that – people are kind of ashamed.' At this school, the priority was discretion, in order to help families access the food bank.

At Booth Primary School, the priority was to reduce stigma through the language used and the operation of the food pantry. The food pantry manager explained that he saw his job as 'reducing that [stigma] as much as possible':

> I think it's not a foodbank, that's the key. There's dignity in the transaction. So, we make them pay £3.50, they have to – some people struggle to pay that and some people pay it easily but the point is they come with dignity, there's dignity in the transaction and they go away with dignity. (Matt, Booth Primary School)

Similarly, at the children's centre, the operation of the food bank as a food pantry with people having to pay for a set amount of food that they chose was seen as reducing the social embarrassment of free food. Stephanie explained, 'the variety makes people feel proud of attending the food pantry, as opposed to ashamed'. The Felix Project in their advice to schools recommends using a food pantry model with choice and donations for this very reason; Felicity explained: 'It's around that choice, that dignity, all that that comes with it not getting a ready-made bag' (Felicity, Felix Project).

At Peabody Primary School, they adopted a range of strategies, based on their knowledge of the parents, to ensure everyone could access the food.

> So some families can be quiet, some are really open and some are quite happy for their children to walk out with their bags of food and to them, that's fine. Other people [say] 'No, what's the quietest part of the day?' And they really want this completely undercover and that's absolutely fine; it's what works for them ... They'll say 'What if I bump into someone I know?' And you see, in school, I'm in control of that because I'll tell you a time and a date to come in. (Lesley, Peabody Primary School)

Lesley explained that they were required to adapt to what families wanted in terms of openness, and that they were able to reassure parents by giving them a set time to visit.

These strategies were based on schools' knowledge of the local community and their needs; for example, at Rowntree Primary, the widespread level of deprivation in the local area meant that they wanted the majority of the parents to access the food stall. Even then, there were differences in approaches from parents, as Catherine explained: 'we've got some families that would have, you know whatever's on offer they would happily take, and we've got others that are horrified and almost have been heartbroken about having to do it [use the food stall]'. While the general and open provision at Rowntree worked for them, in most other schools, it was important that the division between those needing the food and those not was not obvious.

The context of the local community was important in making these decisions, as was the growing need that meant more and more families required support. Audrey at Field Nursery School argued that there was actually far less stigma about needing food during the cost-of-living crisis than before; she said 'people are more willing to talk about it now, there isn't that stigma attached as much as there used to be before'. Public awareness, she argued, was also important; she noted, 'even in supermarkets and stuff like that now you have Felix, the posters, the promotional stuff is there and it's just more of that, you know, "You can reach out to us if you need help"'. For Audrey, a combination of the Covid crisis and greater promotion of food waste organisations have contributed to a reduction in stigma and families being more willing to ask for help. Building on the improved relationships discussed earlier in this chapter, families are also more willing to ask those that they trust and know well for help when they are struggling. Charlotte at Rowntree Primary made a similar observation: 'I think more and more are open to talking about it. There's not as much, and there's shouldn't be, but that pride or shame. I see very little of that, very little.'

At the same time, as Audrey noted, the greater public awareness of systems of sharing waste food make the whole enterprise less Othering for families. At Webb Primary School, their 'eco' approach also meant a generalised reduction in stigma. Genevieve and Grace compared the parents who refused a Christmas hamper because they 'didn't want to be seen walking out with these plastic bags with their name on it', with the food bank where 'they all bring their own bags or they bring their trolleys, don't they, and it just looks better for the children'. Genevieve explained 'it's a bit different these days, like people aren't as ashamed. Because we also sell it as though "come and save the planet"', also arguing that 'I don't think people are shy to come when it's about saving the environment'.

The schools in our sample were working hard, in multiple different ways, to increase access to their food bank, both in practical terms and in social terms, by reducing the stigma attached. These practical justifications for having the food bank at the school were linked to the moral justifications in that the staff seemed to reason that if the school had to operate a food bank, it needed to be effective.

Conclusion

This chapter has set out the reasons why schools operate food banks, in terms of the benefits to them as educational institutions, and the reasons why schools are an ideal site for food provision. In answer to the question of what is in it for them, we argue that schools benefit hugely from the increased learning and reduced stress (discussed in Chapter Four), and the improved relationships with parents. The sense of trust and connectedness fostered by the food bank has a dual advantage, in that it allows the staff to help children better in school as they are more aware of their needs, and allows the food bank to be operated in ways which best help families. The food bank does have an impact on parent and staff subjectivities, as the power relationships between the two are shifted, and there are some difficulties in relationships with parents caused by the food bank.

Our participants give an account of the reasons for operating a food bank based on moral obligations, the fact that they are faced with hungry children and have a human instinct to care and help, as well as a professional commitment to care. They feel responsible for solving the problem of hungry families, in the absence of any other option. The practical and social advantages of locating the food bank at school, where it is convenient for families and less stigmatising than a public food bank, add to the sense that school staff simply want to help solve the problem of poverty as much as they can. They have good knowledge of the local families, and so can adapt their approach to providing food based on what they know parents will access. Schools are thus an ideal site for food banks for families, given the expertise of the staff and easy location. What this does not necessarily mean, however, is that schools *should* be the site for food banks, merely that they have become a good solution to a problem. In the next chapter, we focus on this process of responsibilisation, and consider what it means for the education sector.

SIX

Where is policy? Schools, responsibility and the withdrawal of the state

Introduction

In this chapter, we consider the wider policy implications of food banks and other welfare-centred work in schools, and return to our central argument relating to the responsibilisation of schools to address the problem of child poverty. We begin with a discussion of the research data collected on staff views of food banks as a phenomenon, and their arguments in relation to who is responsible for feeding hungry families. We also consider the impact on budgets and staff, and the lack of recognition for this work within accountability systems. This leads into a more detailed examination of the political debate over where the responsibility for addressing families' increasing needs lies, and whether education should be the location of welfare services. We consider here the potential for growing disparities between schools, if schools are made responsible for feeding families. We focus on the lack of policy in this area for schools, and the lack of recognition and funding of this work. Part of this discussion considers how tools from policy sociology relating to how policy is enacted by schools are insufficient to understand this topic, so we need to evolve these to consider how schools act when faced with a policy vacuum.

We then examine the issue of responsibility in more depth, by considering whether the argument made in relation to public food banks and the withdrawal of the state applies to school food banks. We consider the tensions between an argument that describes the state as withdrawing from responsibility, and the phenomenon of schools as state institutions becoming instead responsible for providing food. This leads us to argue for a more nuanced understanding of how responsibilisation is operating within the neoliberal state. The chapter concludes with a discussion of how we might conceptualise educational responses to the cost-of-living crisis, and why this research matters in terms of how we view schools and the welfare state.

The wider policy context

In these final discussions of the research data, we consider the wider policy context in which these schools operate, and participants' views of where responsibility should lie for providing food for families in need. One clear explanation for the need for food banks, in addition to those already discussed, was based on the problems caused by wider social policy, including benefit changes, and the retrenchment of public services. At Twining Primary School, Sarah commented:

> Schools are being asked to hold families more and more and more often. So for example, the child and adolescent mental health unit has got an 18-month waiting list and we could have children that are actually self-harming. And we're having to hold those children because of the waiting list. We've got children and parents that are on waiting lists for treatment at hospitals – and staff as well. And it's not right. We're holding these families and trying to keep them going and keep them going, and

keep them going and keep them going. The food bank is another side to that.

The school is 'keeping families going' in the face of waits for mental health appointments or for medical treatment, Sarah explains, with the food bank being part of that package of support. She is acutely aware of the impact of reduced other services on how families can function, and in this context the food bank is needed to ease one of the most pressing problems.

Grace at Booth Primary School made a similar point about the additional things that schools are doing to resolve problems associated with housing and increased energy bills:

> I'm happy to do it and I enjoy doing it, but it's not acceptable and it makes me really sad that we have to. But we will carry on doing it. Because like we shouldn't have to offer free wraparound. We shouldn't have to write letters about housing. We shouldn't have to worry about being closed because of the strike day, that children aren't going to be warm. It's completely unacceptable.

As Grace explains, these are things that the school 'should not have to worry about', but they do. She is concerned that children will be cold in their homes when the school is shut for one day for a national teachers' strike; this is 'completely unacceptable', but they will carry on. In Grace's explanation, 'we have to', because of the wider needs of the community.

In some cases, there was real despondency about the lack of recognition of the scale of child poverty and the effectiveness of measures to reduce it:

> I still don't think a lot of people realise how widespread it is and how many people it does affect. Yes, I know it's all relative isn't it, but I still don't think that even things that get put out there, say, so that are meant to

> help families and they're meant to do this, I think there's always something in it that means that actually, it isn't really helping them. Or, yes, that might help that, but then you're actually at the detriment of something else. So I don't really see any end to it [food banks] anytime soon, unless there's some big changes much higher than the level we're working at, no. (Bethany, Dimbleby Nursery)

For Bethany, the level of change needed is 'much higher' than that of the school; in other words, decisions need to be made at a national or local government level in order to resolve the poverty that she sees. Helen at Brown Pre-School similarly argued that change 'has to come from obviously the top'. Without wider recognition, Bethany comments, this seems unlikely, and the measures taken either do not help families, or do help, but at the expense of something else. There is no end in sight for the food bank, therefore, without 'big change'.

Some of these more pessimistic viewpoints were related directly to the cost-of-living crisis: the wider economic context of high inflation was identified as the underlying reason why food banks were needed. Natalie at Rashford Nursery School commented that prices 'just keep rising and rising and rising ... but we're not getting the money to pay for it'. This also affected staff, as discussed in Chapter Three, who also needed the food bank at times. These wider contextual issues which the school had no control over, including stagnant wage growth, the reduction in public services and high inflation, left the school with no option but to help families.

The escalation of the cost-of-living crisis, particularly through the winter of 2022–23, was apparent to workers at the Felix Project. Felicity explained: 'I'm really noticing the difference in the year and a half I've worked here from schools, when I started, going, "we want healthy, healthy, healthy", to now, 'We'll take anything. Our families are desperate. They just need food.' While the higher levels of need were apparent in many interviews, there were also longer-term explanations why school food banks are needed, and those that dealt with the politics of child poverty more explicitly. In particular, when we asked participants if schools should have food banks, they often answered first in terms of practicality (usually yes because they are helpful to families); and then some responded further in relation to food banks as a moral and political problem. This second answer was often critical of the decisions made which mean that families live in poverty:

> I don't think we should need to have food banks. Yes, I don't think we should need to, but working with what we've got and the situation that we're in, I do think, yes, if places can do it. (Bethany, Dimbleby Nursery)

> I think the government could probably step in and be a lot more helpful than what they are being nowadays to us and to families. Like I said, if it wasn't for the food banks there would be a lot, lot more people struggling and obviously then it would have a bigger impact, like you said, on the long term on the government and on families' health as well, I definitely do think it would have a knock-on effect. (Audrey, Field Nursery School)

> In an ideal world, no, a school shouldn't have to do a food bank. A need was there. Covid made it happen. That need was probably there 17 years ago when I first got the job here. So, no, no we shouldn't. I don't know what the answer is. (Charlotte, Rowntree Primary School)

> I mean the ideal would be that we don't need to exist ever anyway, but I don't think the cost of living or food poverty as a whole is going anywhere any time soon. (Stephanie, Oliver Children's Centre)

These participants argued that there should not be an underlying need for a food bank – in line with the Trussell Trust's aim for a future without food banks (Bull et al, 2023) – in an ideal world. But the situation that schools are in, with the higher levels of need among families, means that schools are well placed. It is important to emphasise that school staff were aware of the wider context of their work, even though they might not often mention it; they were often angry, or very sad, about the need for the food bank in their school. While many saw a future without food banks as an impossible dream, some suggested potential changes, often in relation to pay and benefits:

> We should live in a society where people actually get paid and everyone can have a job. But unfortunately I don't have a magic wand. (Sophie, Rowntree Primary School)

> The list is endless [of what should change]. I mean, you should put up benefits, you should – I don't know, you should change the system. I think certain systems need re-looking at and so forth … The government could do a lot more. They could do a lot more. But what, I don't know. There's so much that they could do, but more money, it's more money. (Sasha, Twining Primary School)

> I think the area that needs looking at is not necessarily the families on benefits. It's those that are on low-paid work. There are families that are really struggling. (Naomi, Rashford Nursery School)

> I find it disgusting that we're in a state where we can't pay the people a living wage to be able to have that pride of earning money and going to buy your own food. And that we can't support people enough that aren't in the position to work to also just have the dignity of buying their own food. (Greg, Wilson Nursery)

These comments reveal the strength of feeling among some participants about the financial situations faced by some families, and the causes in terms of wages and benefits. As seen in earlier chapters, while there were some deficit views of parents, we also see here how some staff were fully aware of the wider context which leads to food insecurity among families. This policy context was vital in understanding the complicated reasoning behind the schools operating a food bank; in contrast, there was a lack of policy on how schools should be responding, which we focus on next.

Policy enactment, context and the policy vacuum on food insecurity

While schools are affected by legislation on school meals and nutrition, there is little guidance, statutory or otherwise, on how schools should address food insecurity. Many schools offer breakfast clubs, and the Labour government made this statutory in 2024, but the provision of free or subsidised food remains an area where there is a policy vacuum. This leaves some headteachers uncertain about how to manage the financial demands of offering a food bank, and many staff uncertain about whether a school *should* be stepping beyond their educational purpose. This lack of policy mirrors the 'persistent lack of a policy response or effective policy framework taking responsibility for food insecurity' in society more generally (Lambie-Mumford & Loopstra, 2020, p 209).

As we have argued, this vacuum means that the usual ways of conceptualising policy enactment are insufficient for understanding food banks in schools, as schools are not directly responding to policy. There are commonalities here with 'crisis policy enactment' (Bradbury et al, 2022), in that these actions can be conceptualised as a 'response to policy which is focused first on coping but is also agentic, demonstrating a commitment to children's welfare and a belief in the power of schools to make a difference' (p 761). However, those food banks that began before Covid or were set up after, or those that have evolved since their pandemic beginnings, cannot be understood only with recourse to crisis policy enactment. This means that we need to think differently about why and how school do what they do, not just how they 'do policy', but about wider practice. We return to this theme later in the chapter.

That said, we can see how the different contextual dimensions described by Braun et al (2011), and the school staff's perceptions of these contexts, affect *how* the food banks are organised. School food banks are certainly reflective of the values and ethical positions of school leaders (what Braun et al term the *professional* context), as we have seen in the discussions of the need to reduce the stigma faced by families. As we saw in Chapter Five, there was a great sense of the moral need to provide food for hungry children and families. This moral obligation was juxtaposed, by some, with some concern about the school moving beyond its educational purpose:

> I mean, it's way beyond my remit, so to speak, as a headteacher, but when I came into education as a teacher sort of 28 years ago, I wouldn't have expected to run a food bank. I would have expected to do half of the things I'm doing. But I think it's just how things have changed. But particularly schools like ours, I think it's a good thing. (Sasha, Twining Primary School)

> Yes, I think they ought to be there, but no I don't think it ought to be down to schools to provide them. We do it because there's a need, but it's not our job to feed the children in the community. Our job is to look after them and educate them and care for them while they're at school, not to feed them at the weekends or holidays, but we can't help but be concerned about that. (Catherine, Rowntree Primary School)

> It's really hard, isn't it? Probably not [schools shouldn't have them] but someone's got to do it, haven't they? Unfortunately, at the moment, we live in a time where

they're needed and if we don't do it, who will? We have the children for the majority of their days with us, this is their safe space and if we are lucky that we have staff and parents who can afford to contribute to that, so we shouldn't have to do it but it needs to happen. (Lorraine, Peabody Primary School)

This view, more common among the headteachers of primary schools, saw the job of feeding children as 'beyond their remit', but as something that was necessary. Sophie, a class teacher, also argued, 'I don't know what would happen if we didn't have all that.' These quotes refocus attention on the child, and the fact that school may be their 'safe space'. This perspective reflects a particular context for the school – where a combination of the ethical stance by the head, and the local (or *situated*) context of high need – means that the school simply has to run a food bank. Unlike some the respondents who thought food banks in schools were a 'good thing' because they improved access, these respondents are unsure about the widening sense of responsibility for social problems.

One exception to this concern was Michael, the head at Booth Primary School, who had a vision for schools as centres of their community, which embraced the wider role of schools, saying, 'schools should sit as the centre of communities that offer a whole range of services':

I would advocate GPs being based in schools, I would advocate all sorts of things being based here because this is the centre where ... We have 700 people come here every single day, 700 parents come here every day so if they can access all of those Job Centre Plus type activities, child care, children's centre type activities, if they can access it all here it's going to be more readily accessible and going to be used by more people than going elsewhere.

Here, Michael sets out the logic of locating other services as well as the food bank at the school site, where many parents visit every day, which would increase use. Michael went on to note that schools are good at identifying the families in need and helping them 'in a dignified way'. For him, the move to provide more on the school site responds well to the community's needs; this may be reflective of the community where his school is located, with high proportions of parents who do not speak English and may be reluctant to visit other places.

The responses from some early years settings also identified the need to care for the whole community in their explanations of why the food bank was needed, particularly Naomi from Rashford Nursery School:

> I'm quite proud of my staff and how they've responded to the issues ... I think it shows that there's still a lot of community spirit out there. And I think maybe that's maybe a positive of Covid, that people have kind of been a bit more community-minded coming out of it and thinking about other people.

The closer links between nurseries and parents compared to primary schools perhaps also facilitate this community spirit and desire to help local families; at Rashford Nursery School, the food bank operates because of the *situated* context of a close-knit community.

School food banks are also affected by what Braun et al call the *material* contexts of policy enactment – 'staffing, budget, buildings, technology and infrastructure' (2011, p 588). Budgetary issues, in particular, were frequently described as limiting what could be offered. The impact on budgets was seen as a major disadvantage of operating a food bank, as money was spent on equipment, staffing and, of course, food:

As much as we really want to do it with the way things are at the moment we're really having to watch what we're spending. (Helen, Brown Pre-School)

Many, many factors to do with numbers [of children] and also like our energy costs and all of those kinds of things to run the building mean that we don't get enough money from the government to make enough money to run the building, so it is a bit tricky ... Mostly I'd say the budget covers it [the food] but the problem is, if I'm completely honest, we don't necessarily get that money in our bank account to then pay them, we have to pay them and then recoup it when they give it to us. Those kinds of things happen a lot but when you don't actually have any money in the bank in order to pay out that can be really tricky where finances are concerned. (Abigail, Field Nursery School)

Schools were affected by rising costs during this period as well as families, including high energy bills and rising food prices. They often relied on donations, including from staff and local businesses. At Dimbleby Nursery, as mentioned previously, there were concerns over the quality and range of food on offer, due to reduced budgets, and this caused problems with the parents who used the food bank. Across the schools, there were significant costs incurred, including for equipment to store food safely, and particularly the staff time involved:

It does have an impact [on staff time], but I don't think any of us could think about stopping it at the moment. I don't think we are that kind of school. (Catherine, Rowntree Primary School)

It can take a lot of time, especially when need changes. So whereas we were doing the food bank and that was sorted as such, we do the weekly shop in order for the things that we need, and then we realised that actually, we need shoes. The children need shoes as well, coats. So it's when you identify a new area of need that it then takes longer, again, more time, but we are lucky, like I say, to have [partnership manager] because she does a lot of the running around, trying to find everyone ... That does take up quite a lot of time, just sending out emails and being told no. (Bethany, Dimbleby Nursery)

I guess it is about that time, we're reaching well beyond our core purpose as a school and when resources are stretched to deliver even our core purpose to try and do the over and above is also a challenge. So we do a lot of fundraising to make sure that we can bring the funds in to keep the staffing levels adequate to be able to deliver these over and above things. Also storage space and space is at a premium, so I think it's all budgetary pressures that are the negatives. (Michael, Booth Primary School)

Because there is a policy vacuum, and providing food is 'beyond our core purpose', the schools have to absorb the costs of time and equipment into their budgets, or engage in fundraising activities. They also have to spend more time on trying to get grants and emailing potential sources, adding further to workloads. Several food banks relied on volunteers in some way, and this was particularly the case for the food pantry run at Oliver Children's Centre:

What we do would never be able to happen if it wasn't for the generosity of our volunteers. Our volunteers are all people that live in the community as well and 90 per cent of our volunteers also access our services. So they are people who have lived experience, and I think that almost emphasises the importance of support. Yes, helping each other out, but it just demonstrates that without volunteers, there's no chance that we'd be able to deliver our projects to the scale that we can because we haven't got the funding, because we haven't got the support from the government. (Stephanie, Oliver Children's Centre)

While this food pantry at the children's centre was funded by the local authority, it still relied heavily on volunteers to function.

We can conclude that the absence of legislation or even guidance on how to manage food insecurity within the school community is important in understanding how food banks in schools operate and how they affect other aspects of school life. Food banks operate both within and as a consequence of this policy vacuum, which is linked to a wider 'policy void' in relation to food insecurity (Lambie-Mumford, 2017). Yet, policy enactment is useful in exploring why schools operate their food banks in different ways, and indeed why they began them. The lack of financial support is a major problem for schools, meaning that food banks are often precarious forms of provision. This failure to support schools financially is inextricably linked with the failure to recognise this work in wider accountability systems.

Accountability and the potential for growing disparities

Schools and nurseries are subject to the accountability framework in England, which is largely formed of Ofsted, the inspectorate and assessment results. In primary schools, there are inspections and test results from SATs at age 10/11 are used to compare and rank schools. In early years, there is a set curriculum and a framework which staff are required to use to assess children, and settings are regularly inspected. The key difference is that nurseries do not have their results published, and they are not related to their Ofsted grade; we therefore focus mainly on the primary schools in this section.

Neither of these forms of accountability recognise the work done by schools to alleviate family food insecurity, our primary school participants argued. Catherine at Rowntree Primary

School argued that 'it won't have an impact on our SATs results or things like that that might put us in a league table', but it improved relationships. Other headteachers agreed:

> It's really hard because we're dedicating time to something like this but if Ofsted came in, I mean, I'd like to think that a well-rounded Ofsted inspector would see this as part of our whole community offering and what value it brings. But it doesn't feature anywhere on the Ofsted framework and the wrong Ofsted inspector may say, actually, why are dedicating your time to that you should be dedicating it onto better maths and reading results. (Michael, Booth Primary School)

> [Ofsted were] very complimentary about everything we do, but they're not interested in your food bank. And actually, they would be almost critical of it if you talked about that, trying to 'make an excuse' – in their words – for other things. So it's almost like you've got to just do it and not talk about it to the people who are holding you to account. Because they would say 'well, that's distracting you from reading results in Year 6'. (Andrea, Lansbury Primary School)

Because of the high stakes nature of Ofsted judgements and tests results for primary schools (Wyse et al, 2022; Perryman et al, 2023), the lack of recognition for the food bank matters highly. Instead of feeling this work is valued, these headteachers fear that the food bank will be criticised as a distraction, or an 'excuse'. As a result, Andrea says that means you 'just do it and not talk about it to the people who are holding you to account'. This lack of recognition is an important backdrop to thinking about how schools run their food banks, as an almost secret operation to help families in need away from the prying eyes of inspectors. In contrast, the early years settings did not mention Ofsted or assessments.

The lack of recognition also matters in that it reflects a wider lack of concern for the context of the school within accountability systems, as found in research on Ofsted (Perryman et al, 2023). The accountability system is something 'done to' schools, rather than for them or with them; it exists almost in a parallel universe to the responsive, community-embedded schools which care about hungry families. But a lack of recognition also risks the widening of disparities, as some schools spend time and energy on projects such as food banks, while others in more affluent areas do not need to. As Sophie at Twining Primary School explained, the money spent on the food bank could be spent on '[r]aising attainment in phonics or an extra member of staff in Year 4 or something'. Time spent on the food banks could be spent improving pupils' attainment in maths and English, as suggested previously. Thus, a systematic failure to recognise this work also fails to recognise the privileges enjoyed by schools which do not need to operate a food bank, because there is no local need. These schools have more time to improve results, the budgets to buy resources, and the time and energy to engage in other activities that enrich children's lives in schools. This is not to say that our case study schools did not attempt these things, but that with a finite set of resources, those schools that do not have to run a food bank simply have more.

It might be argued that the Pupil Premium funding compensates schools for this disparity in what they are required to do. However, our participants saw this funding as insufficient, and as it only relates to children on free school meals, as not recognising the growing need among working families not in receipt of free school meals (FSM). Andrea at Lansbury Primary School explained that there is a 'whole layer of kids under that level who are poverty-stricken, I would say, and who don't get benefits', while Charlotte explained that the 20 per cent of children at Rowntree Primary not on FSM 'will have even less money in the house ... They're our working poor, like our single mums'. Thus, Pupil Premium money did not take into account the needs of families beyond FSM status, and was thus not enough, even in schools with very high FSM rates. Andrea also explained that Pupil Premium money was spent on teaching assistant salaries, not the food bank; the money was already allocated to efforts to reduce the disadvantage gap, even before the need for food banks.

Therefore, the potential for schools spending time and money on providing a food bank to be systematically disadvantaged by the lack of recognition and lack of funding for this work is significant. The policy vacuum around alleviating food insecurity among families does not mean that schools do nothing, as we have seen throughout. Schools' work on food insecurity cannot be acknowledged in a way that is beneficial for the school; because it takes place in a policy vacuum, it is not captured by any system of accountability. We turn now to how we conceptualise this process where schools feel they have to step in, even though this work is not funded or recognised within accountability systems.

The responsibilisation of schools

Throughout this book, we have referred to the responsibilisation of schools to address the consequences of child poverty. We use this term specifically here, in order to frame the discussions about food insecurity within wider discussions of poverty (Lambie-Mumford & Silvasti, 2020). As discussed in Chapter One, the term 'responsibilisation' is used in slightly different ways in educational and social policy scholarship, and here we want to bring these conceptualisations together in order to understand how and why schools have come to operate food banks.

Responsibilisation is usually used within educational scholarship to discuss the permeation of neoliberal expectations that each individual must work hard and be responsible for their own success, within a meritocratic system (Halse et al, 2017). Drawing on governmentality literature based on the work of Foucault, responsibilisation in education is about how headteachers are made responsible for the success of their schools (Keddie, 2015), how teachers are made responsible for school performance at the same time as inclusion (Done & Murphy, 2018), and young people are made responsible for their own educational outcomes, through a 'project of self' (Redmond et al, 2022). This includes showing resilience and 'grit', and being healthy and happy (Jones & Bailey, 2022; Quick, 2024b). Responsibilisation in education literature is thus more about the individual than organisations taking responsibility, but we wish to extend this responsibilisation to the level of the school.

In contrast, the literature on food charity uses the term to examine the way in which the state has absolved itself of responsibility for hungry families, and instead allowed charities and civic society to take responsibility for social problems (Riches, 2020). This is part of a depoliticisation of hunger, so that it becomes a problem for charities to solve, rather than a problem to be solved by increasing benefits, for example.

What we wish to argue, drawing on both of these uses, is that schools have become responsibilised to step in where the state is lacking (the latter usage), but that there are connections with the former conceptualisation, because schools are being forced to take responsibility for the child's wellbeing and welfare. Schools have become in recent years responsible for the whole child as a project of improvement: feeding children, and feeding their families, is an extension of this responsibility for the child as a whole. At the same time, schools become part of the network of food provision which fills the void left when the neoliberal state withdraws from providing adequately for poorer members of society; they are responsibilised in both senses.

A key part of responsibilisation within governmentality literature is individualisation, which might appear to go against the social and relational aspects of schools operating food banks. Individual responsibility discourses present people as responsible for themselves, and they are therefore expected to bear the consequences. Help is worth giving to those who help themselves, whereas those who do not help themselves (for example, those who spend their money on drugs and alcohol rather than food) are not seen as worthy cases; the old narrative of deservingness persists (Garthwaite, 2017; Tarkiainen, 2022). We see echoes of these discourses within our participants' responses, where school staff comment on the need to give food rather than money, as money might not be spent on buying food for the children, for example. We also saw how parents were framed by some through deficit discourses about poor food choices. Participants were at times quite scathing about parents' failure to help themselves, while there was much enthusiasm from some for projects which would 'empower' parents to manage their finances better, as though management was the main source of the problem. Certainly, the idea of individual responsibility was present in our interviews, but it was far less significant than a discourse of collective responsibility. The staff in our case study schools saw broader social responsibility as important, describing a sense of obligation to help those in need. The driving force behind much of the welfare provision we saw was an alternative discourse, an ethics of care, through which leaders in particular justified their decisions to prioritise the food banks. The overriding justification was the need to address the problem in front of them: the hungry child, the child with falling-apart shoes, the child worried their mum was not eating enough or the child who faced huge stresses as home due to lack of money. The ethics of care, at this point, override the political questions of who is responsible, and instead force the educators to organise food and other provisions within the school setting.

So, how to characterise this shift in terms of responsibilisation? If the food banks were always a result of Covid, then we could see this development as a pandemic-induced new confidence in solving wider problems; an exasperated decision in the midst of a crisis to help families out, a form of crisis policy enactment, which they were never able to step back from. This was the case, we should note, in some schools, reflecting the argument that the pandemic paved the way for a wider sense of social responsibility within the education sector (Baker & Bakopoulou, 2022). In this way, some food banks were a response to a crisis that never stopped, which triggered a sense of collective endeavour within a shared sense of humanity under threat that continued well into the mid-2020s. This was one of Bradbury's 'post-pandemic hopes', that we might 'take the collectivity, empathy and care shown during the pandemic into the future' (2021, p 139).

However, many of the food banks in our case study schools dated to the pre-Covid era, and cannot be attributed to a slippage of responsibilities during the pandemic or a crisis mentality. Instead, like wider food bank culture in the UK, they date back to the early 2010s and the period of austerity, and can be related to changes in welfare benefits. Food banks – in schools and in wider society – can only be understood as part of pre-existing responses to a wider shift in responsibility from the state to the individual, we would argue. Food banks in schools are not the same as public food banks, however, in a number of important ways; significantly, they are state funded, so when they operate a food bank to address the withdrawal of the state, they are in fact an example of the state still taking responsibility, however indirectly. It does not make sense to talk about the withdrawal of the state if it is a state institution addressing the problem. We cannot simply lump school food banks in with food banks in general, in how we understand their role within a process of state retrenchment. This contradiction and the unique position of school food banks can be explained by the importance of the ethics of care to teachers and education leaders; and it can also be seen as related to the view of schools as responsible for the whole child – as in Jones' (2021) argument that neoliberal governance has extended to the 'emotional and moral life of the child'.

This conceptualisation of school food banks as representing a state-funded solution to a state-produced problem takes into account the strength of feeling of our participants about the importance of care in their roles. We would argue that what the political economy analysis does not account for, in this case, is the professional identity of teachers as caring individuals. Faced with hungry or worried children, school leaders have chosen to act, in order to alleviate this problem. This agency is exercised due to human need, which has of course in turn been caused by welfare retrenchment. In stepping in, schools are not necessarily engaging with the neoliberal project of depoliticising hunger in quite the same way as the public food bank organisations. Providing food is not their *raison d'être*, but an add-on that they feel morally obliged to organise.

We can understand the food banks in schools phenomenon as the state withdrawing, and another arm of the state expanding so that it reaches far enough to fill (some of) the void that is left, because that arm of the state is one defined by an ethics of care. We might see more recent expansion of food banks in the NHS (Bryant, 2023) as analogous to this. Our argument here aligns in some ways with that of social geographers Cloke et al (2017), in their discussion of alternative ways of conceptualising public food banks as 'spaces of care, and as liminal spaces of encounter capable of incubating political and ethical values, practices and subjectivities that challenge neoliberal austerity' (2017, p 703). This more hopeful argument acknowledges that food banks may be a 'serious barrier in the fight against poverty', but that says that hegemonic applications of these perspectives are too simplistic – as if 'no possible good can be seen in them' (p 706). Instead, 'these seemingly mundane spaces of care and welfare can serve as potentially virtuous arenas of common life' (p 708), where people from different backgrounds encounter one another. Food banks without vouchers (like the school ones discussed here), and those that emphasise reducing the stigma experienced by families, represent for Cloke et al an alternative to the common perception of food banks as enabling a denuded welfare state to function. We make a similar argument here that food banks in schools represent a challenge to neoliberal individualism and the reduced state, at the same time as they enable the retrenchment of public services and are an example of neoliberal responsibilisation.

Food banks in schools are examples of responsibilisation, in that they are there because the state has absolved itself of providing enough support for families with low incomes, but they are also evidence of how the education sector responds when faced with needs. Thus, we would argue that in order to understand food banks in schools we need a more nuanced understanding of how responsibilisation is operating within the neoliberal state.

Conclusion

In his discussion of the international research evidence on food banks, Riches argues that this work provokes the question of 'who benefits and why from these particular social and political arrangements as the front-line response to poverty' (2020, p XIV). In this book, we have begun to explore who benefits from the arrangement of schools offering food to families, while bearing in mind the significance of this as a political arrangement. We have explored benefits for the schools, and their perceptions of the benefits for families, though this latter area is one which merits far more detailed attention by researchers. What Riches is suggesting, however, is that there are beneficiaries of this state of affairs, where charitable organisations resolve the problem of hunger, rather than the state taking responsibility. Food banks shift our understanding of the state, as part of an individualising message that says, 'If you are struggling, that is your individual responsibility, but if you are hungry, charities will come to your aid.' They shape how we understand need, and those who deserve help, as we have seen in the deficit discourses deployed by some of our participants.

Certainly, food banks in schools are part of this problematic solution to poverty, as they too fill a gap which then remains unrecognised. But as we have seen throughout this book, they are more than that too, representing evidence of the human desire to help those in need, based on close relationships with children and their families and a detailed understanding of the local community. They are also hugely helpful, in that there is a reduced stigma attached to a food bank in a school, and perhaps they are therefore more effective in solving the problem of hunger than public food banks.

The story of school food banks is therefore in many ways a positive one: they are highly effective in helping families, ideally situated and associated with less stigma and shame; they help strengthen relationships between school and parents, and allow schools to better understand families' needs; they help children to learn, and to participate with dignity in everyday childhood activities. Food banks can be seen as part of a school's commitment to inclusion. They can be seen as the response of an ethically-driven, caring profession to a real need that they are confronted with on a daily basis, in a context where the state has allowed child poverty to rise and there is no policy on what schools should do in response.

But there is a more negative story to be told too: the abdication of responsibility for feeding families by the state is alarming, and the normalisation of child poverty to an extent that the thought for these staff of stopping their food bank is abhorrent. Making schools responsible for the child as a whole is problematic. The operation of a food bank is not without costs: there are impacts on some relationships between school and families, and they can be a space where parents are judged or disapproved of for their personal choices. Moreover, food banks have a significant impact in terms of time and money, and they are not recognised within the accountability framework, leaving some schools faced with an uneven burden of alleviating food insecurity. This risks the entrenchment of disparities between schools in more disadvantaged areas and others, as the more affluent schools enjoy the luxury of more time and funding. Food banks in schools are not sustainable in their present form.

This leaves us with the question of whether schools *should* have food banks, which we asked all our participants. In our view, the problem of child poverty and food insecurity would ideally be reduced to an extent that food banks are not needed, but if the current level of need is to persist, then one of two options is necessary. First, the state could fund this form of welfare work, through significantly increased funding to schools in areas of high poverty, including providing capital funding for the buildings and equipment necessary to provide a food bank in an effective and dignified way for parents. This would be a major investment in schools and nurseries as centres for the whole family, which would mark a significant shift in how the education sector functions and its core purpose. Second, this provision could exist elsewhere, operating in ways which offer the same advantages as food banks in schools – easy access, lack of stigma, no eligibility requirements and a prioritisation of families – though this would be a challenge to achieve. Neither situation is preferable to the ideal of reducing child poverty overall, and both include significant challenges. But one or the other needs to be achieved if families are to be helped to access food in a sustainable way. We hope the Labour government who took power in the final stages of writing this book will take this issue seriously.

As Baker et al (2024) have argued, a significant proportion of the food bank sector in England is operating within schools, but this is overlooked in many discussions of food charity. What we hope to have contributed within this book is a detailed consideration of the phenomenon of food banks in schools and nurseries, from the perspective of how these fit with the existing scholarship on schools, and the perspective of thinking about food banks and the neoliberal state. The food banks in schools within our case studies are examples of both human generosity and professional expertise, and of a deeply worrying level of child poverty and lack of support for families. We hope that, at the very least, we can draw attention to the existence of food banks in school and thus increase awareness of the level of child poverty present in England.

Notes on anti-poverty and food campaigners

Historical

Charles Booth (1840–1916) was a social researcher and reformer, famous for mapping the levels of poverty in London.

George Lansbury (1859–1940) was a social reformer and a politician, who was leader of the Labour Party from 1932 to 1935.

George Peabody (1795–1869) was an American who lived in London and tackled poverty through provision of low-rent housing.

Joseph Rowntree (1836–1925) was a social reformer who set up the Joseph Rowntree Foundation to address the root causes of social problems.

Louisa Twining (1820–1912) was a philanthropist and campaigner on issues relating to the Poor Law.

Martha Beatrice Webb (1858–1943) was a sociologist and social reformer, who co-founded the London School of Economics.

Contemporary

Gordon Brown (1951–) is a former Labour Prime Minister who since leaving office in 2010 has campaigned on the issue of child poverty.

NOTES ON ANTI-POVERTY AND FOOD CAMPAIGNERS

Henry Dimbleby (1970–) is a businessman and cookery writer who has campaigned on school food and led the National Food Strategy, which included recommendations on helping disadvantaged children.

Frank Field (1942–2024) was a Labour MP and minister, and later a cross-bench life peer, who campaigned on welfare reform.

Jamie Oliver (1975–) is a well-known chef who has led campaigns on healthy school food and children's nutrition.

Marcus Rashford (1997–) is a Premier League and England footballer who has led prominent campaigns on the need to reduce child hunger.

Bex Wilson is a teacher in Leeds who set up a charity which provides beds for children without one.

Note

For clarity, use of these names as pseudonyms does not indicate support for all their views or actions; we merely wished to use names associated with the issues raised in the book.

References

Anderson, S. A. (1990). Core indicators of nutritional state for difficult-to-sample populations. *The Journal of Nutrition*, *120* (11), 1555–98.

Baker, W. (2023). Schools and food charity in England. *British Educational Research Journal*, *49*(6), 1387–402.

Baker, W., & Bakopoulou, I. (2022). Children's centres, families and food insecurity in times of crisis. *Journal of Poverty & Social Justice*, *31*(13), 1–18.

Baker, W., Knight, C., & Leckie, G. (2024). Feeding hungry families: food banks in schools in England. Bristol Working Papers in Education. Retrieved 3 April 2024 from https://www.bristol.ac.uk/media-library/sites/education/documents/bristol-working-papers-in-education/Baker_Feeding%20Hungry%20Families%20Food%20Banks%20in%20Schools%20in%20England.pdf

Ball, S. (2013). *Foucault, power and education*. Routledge.

Ball, S. J. (2021). *The education debate*. Policy Press.

Beck, D., & Gwilym, H. (2020). The moral maze of food bank use. *Journal of Poverty & Social Justice*, *28*(3), 383–99.

Belger, T. (2022). Schools now 'part of the welfare state' as cost of living crisis deepens. Schools Week. Retrieved 24 July 2024 from https://schoolsweek.co.uk/schools-now-part-of-the-welfare-state-as-cost-of-living-crisis-deepens/

BERA (2018). *Ethical guidelines for educational research* (4th edn). British Educational Research Association.

REFERENCES

Berman, Y., & Hovland, T. (2024). The cost of austerity: how UK public spending cuts led to 190,000 excess deaths. LSE Blogs. Retrieved 20 September 2024 from https://blogs.lse.ac.uk/inequalities/2024/06/19/the-cost-of-austerity-how-spending-cuts-led-to-190000-excess-deaths

Billington, T. (2017). Educational inclusion and critical neuroscience: friends or foes? *International Journal of Inclusive Education, 21*(8), 866–80.

Bishop, N. (2023). *Parent partnership in the primary school: a practical guide for school leaders and other key staff*. Routledge.

Bogiatzis-Gibbons, D., Broch-Due, I., Breathnach, S., Evans, A., Gadenne, V., Hardy, T., et al (2021). The National School Breakfast Programme. Retrieved 29 July 2024 from https://www.magicbreakfast.com/wp-content/uploads/2023/11/National-School-Breakfast-Programme.pdf

Bradbury, A. (2019). Making little neo-liberals: the production of ideal child/learner subjectivities in primary school through choice, self-improvement and 'growth mindsets'. *Power & Education, 11*(3), 309–26.

Bradbury, A. (2021). *Ability, inequality and post-pandemic schools: rethinking contemporary myths of meritocracy*. Policy Press.

Bradbury, A., Braun, A., Duncan, S., Harmey, S., Levy, R., & Moss, G. (2022). Crisis policy enactment: primary school leaders' responses to the Covid-19 pandemic in England. *Journal of Education Policy, 38*(1), 1–21.

Bradbury, A., & Roberts-Holmes, G. (2016). Creating an Ofsted story: the role of early years assessment data in schools' narratives of progress. *British Journal of Sociology of Education, 38*(7), 1–10.

Bradbury, A., & Vince, S. (2023). Food banks in schools: educational responses to the cost-of-living crisis. Helen Hamlyn Centre for Pedagogy (0–11 years), UCL Institute of Education. Retrieved 20 September 2024 from https://discovery.ucl.ac.uk/id/eprint/10174817/

Bradbury, A., & Vince, S. (2024). Food banks in early years settings: the impact on children, families and staff. UCL Institute of Education. Retrieved 20 September 2024 from https://discovery.ucl.ac.uk/id/eprint/10185872/1/Food%20banks%20in%20EY%20Bradbury%20Vince.pdf

Braun, A., Ball, S. J., Maguire, M., & Hoskins, K. (2011). Taking context seriously: towards explaining policy enactments in the secondary school. *Discourse: Studies in the Cultural Politics of Education, 32*(4), 585–96.

Braun, A., Maguire, M., & Ball, S. (2012). *How schools do policy: policy enactments in secondary schools*. Routledge.

Brown, S. M., Doom, J. R., Lechuga-Peña, S., Watamura, S. E., & Koppels, T. (2020). Stress and parenting during the global COVID-19 pandemic. *Child Abuse & Neglect, 110*(Pt 2), 104699.

Bruer, J. T. (1999). *The myth of the first three years: a new understanding of early brain development and lifelong learning*. Simon & Schuster.

Bryant, M. (2023). Half of NHS trusts providing or planning food banks for staff. *The Guardian*. Retrieved 1 August 2024 from https://www.theguardian.com/business/2023/jan/08/nhs-trusts-hospitals-food-banks-for-staff-nurses

Bull, R., Miles, C., Newbury, E., Nichols, A., Weekes, T., & Wyld, G. (2023). Hunger in the UK. The Trussell Trust. Retrieved 29 July 2024 from https://www.trussell.org.uk/publications/hunger-in-the-uk

Busby, E. (2018). Thousands of headteachers march on Westminster over school funding 'crisis'. *The Independent*. Retrieved 29 July 2024 from https://www.independent.co.uk/news/education/education-news/headteachers-westminster-march-school-funding-cuts-budget-austerity-worthless-campaign-a8558996.html

Busso, D. S., & Pollack, C. (2015). No brain left behind: consequences of neuroscience discourse for education. *Learning, Media & Technology, 40*(2), 168–86.

Caraher, M., & Furey, S. (2017). Is it appropriate to use surplus food to feed people in hunger? Short-term Band-Aid to more deep rooted problems of poverty. Food Research Collaboration Policy Brief. Retrieved 28 July 2024 from https://foodresearch.org.uk/publications/is-it-appropriate-to-use-surplus-food-to-feed-people-in-hunger/

Chefs in Schools (2022). Survation chefs in schools 2022 survey. Chefs in Schools. Retrieved 29 July 2024 from https://chefsinschools.org.uk/wp-content/uploads/2022/10/Chefs-in-Schools-Summary.pdf

REFERENCES

Cloke, P., May, J., & Williams, A. (2017). The geographies of food banks in the meantime. *Progress in Human Geography*, *41*(6), 703–26.

Cohen, J. F., Hecht, A. A., McLoughlin, G. M., Turner, L., & Schwartz, M. B. (2021). Universal school meals and associations with student participation, attendance, academic performance, diet quality, food security, and body mass index: a systematic review. *Nutrients*, *13*(3), 911.

Corrie, L. (2000). Neuroscience and early childhood? A dangerous liaison. *Australian Journal of Early Childhood*, *25*(2), 34–40.

CPAG (2023). Official child poverty statistics: 350,000 more children in poverty and numbers will rise. Child Poverty Action Group. Retrieved 29 July 2024 from https://cpag.org.uk/news/offic ial-child-poverty-statistics-350000-more-children-poverty-and-numbers-will-rise

CPAG (2024). Child poverty reaches record high – failure to tackle it will be 'a betrayal of Britain's children'. Child Poverty Action Group. Retrieved 28 July 2024 from https://cpag.org.uk/news/child-poverty-reaches-record-high-failure-tackle-it-will-be-betra yal-britains-children

Crown, H. (2019). Childcare practitioners 'living in poverty' – exclusive survey. Nursery World. Retrieved 28 July 2024 from https://www.nurseryworld.co.uk/news/article/childcare-practi tioners-living-in-poverty-exclusive-survey

Daly, M., & Kelly, G. (2015). *Families and poverty: everyday life on a low income*. Policy Press.

Department for Education (2024). Education provision: children under 5 years of age. GOV.UK. Retrieved 1 August 2024 from https://explore-education-statistics.service.gov.uk/find-statistics/education-provision-children-under-5

Desforges, C., & Abouchaar, A. (2003). *The impact of parental involvement, parental support and family education on pupil achievement and adjustment: a literature review* (Vol. 433). DfES London.

Done, E. J., & Murphy, M. (2018). The responsibilisation of teachers: a neoliberal solution to the problem of inclusion. *Discourse: Studies in the Cultural Politics of Education*, *39*(1), 142–55.

Dowler, E., & Lambie-Mumford, H. (2015). How can households eat in austerity? Challenges for social policy in the UK. *Social Policy & Society*, *14*(3), 417–28.

Drummond, M. J., & Yarker, P. (2013). The enduring problem of fixed ability: but is a new conversation beginning? *FORUM*, *55*(1), 3–7.

Dunifon, R., & Jones, L. (2003). The influences of participation in the National School Lunch Program and food insecurity on child well-being. *Social Service Review*, *77*(1), 72–92.

Earl, L., & Lalli, G. S. (2020). Healthy meals, better learners? Debating the focus of school food policy in England. *British Journal of Sociology of Education*, *41*(4), 476–89.

Early Education (2015). Maintained nursery schools: the state of play. Retrieved 13 August 2018 from https://early-education.org.uk/wp-content/uploads/2021/12/Nursery-Schools-State-of-Play-Report-final-print.pdf

Edwards, J. (2023). An appetite for the system? A critical evaluation of the Dimbleby report. *British Politics*. Retrieved 3 October 2024 from https://doi.org/10.1057/s41293-023-00239-w

EPI (2024). Annual report 2024: disadvantage. Education Policy Institute. Retrieved 30 July 2024 from https://epi.org.uk/annual-report-2024-disadvantage-2/

Felix Project (nd). Our vision/what we do. Retrieved 1 August 2024 from https://thefelixproject.org/about/our-story

Food Foundation (2024). Food insecurity tracking. Retrieved 29 July 2024 from https://foodfoundation.org.uk/initiatives/food-insecurity-tracking

Fotheringham, P., Harriott, T., Healy, G., Arenge, G., & Wilson, E. (2022). Pressures and influences on school leaders navigating policy development during the COVID-19 pandemic. *British Educational Research Journal*, *48*(2), 201–27.

Francis-Devine, B., Malik, X., & Danechi, S. (2023). Food poverty: households, food banks and free school meals. House of Commons Library. Retrieved 29 July 2024 from https://researchbriefings.files.parliament.uk/documents/CBP-9209/CBP-9209.pdf

Garthwaite, K. (2016a). *Hunger pains: life inside foodbank Britain*. Policy Press.

REFERENCES

Garthwaite, K. (2016b). Stigma, shame and 'people like us': an ethnographic study of foodbank use in the UK. *Journal of Poverty & Social Justice*, *24*(3), 277–89.

Garthwaite, K. (2017). Rethinking deservingness, choice and gratitude in emergency food provision. In J. Hudson, C. Needham, & E. Heins (Eds), *Social policy review 29* (pp 87–104). Bristol University Press.

Gaunt, C. (2020). Coronavirus: families on free school meals will be sent vouchers during school closures. Nursery World. Retrieved 13 July 2024 from https://www.nurseryworld.co.uk/news/article/coronavirus-families-on-free-school-meals-will-be-sent-vouchers-during-school-closures

Gooseman, A., Defeyter, M. A., & Graham, P. L. (2020). Hunger in the primary school setting: evidence, impacts and solutions according to school staff in the North East of England, UK. *Education 3–13*, *48*(2), 191–203.

Graham, P. L., & Fenwick, C. (2022). Food insecurity in school-aged children. In W. McGovern, A. Gillespie, & H. Woodley (Eds), *Understanding safeguarding for children and their educational experiences* (pp 151–61). Emerald Publishing.

Gulliford, M. C., Nunes, C., & Rocke, B. (2006). Food insecurity, weight control practices and body mass index in adolescents. *Public Health Nutrition*, *9*(5), 570–4.

Halse, C., Hartung, C., & Wright, J. (2017). Responsibility and responsibilisation in education. *Discourse: Studies in the Cultural Politics of Education*, *38*(1), 1.

Harari, D., Francis-Devine, B., Bolton, P., & Keep, M. (2023). Rising cost of living in the UK. Retrieved 29 July 2024 from https://researchbriefings.files.parliament.uk/documents/CBP-9428/CBP-9428.pdf

Harmey, S., & Moss, G. (2023). Learning disruption or learning loss: using evidence from unplanned closures to inform returning to school after COVID-19. *Educational Review*, *75*(4), 637–56.

Hoskins, K., Bradbury, A., & Fogarty, L. (2021). A frontline service? Nursery schools as local community hubs in an era of austerity. *Journal of Early Childhood Research*, *19*(3), 355–68.

IFS (2021). Annual report on education spending in England. Institute for Fiscal Studies. Retrieved 22 July 2024 from https://ifs.org.uk/publications/2021-annual-report-education-spending-england

Jones, B. M. A. (2021). *Educating the neoliberal whole child: a genealogical approach*. Routledge.

Jones, B. M. A., & Bailey, P. (2022). Character as calculable: the performative and biopolitical management of the child's soul. In M. Tamboukou (Ed), *Thinking with Stephen J. Ball: lines of flight in education* (pp 16–34). Routledge.

JRF (2023). 'Heart-breaking and wrong' that a million children under 4 growing up in poverty. Retrieved 29 July 2024 from https://www.jrf.org.uk/news/heart-breaking-and-wrong-that-a-million-children-under-4-growing-up-in-poverty-jrf

Ke, J., & Ford-Jones, E. L. (2015). Food insecurity and hunger: a review of the effects on children's health and behaviour. *Paediatrics & Child Health*, *20*(2), 89–91.

Keddie, A. (2015). New modalities of state power: neoliberal responsibilisation and the work of academy chains. *International Journal of Inclusive Education*, *19*(11), 1190–205.

Keddie, A. (2016). Children of the market: performativity, neoliberal responsibilisation and the construction of student identities. *Oxford Review of Education*, 42(1), 108–22.

Knight, A., O'Connell, R., & Brannen, J. (2018). Eating with friends, family or not at all: young people's experiences of food poverty in the UK. *Children & Society*, *32*(3), 185–94.

Konzelmann, S. J. (2019). *Austerity*. John Wiley & Sons.

Kral, T. V. E., Heo, M., Whiteford, L. M., & Faith, M. S. (2012). Effects on cognitive performance of eating compared with omitting breakfast in elementary schoolchildren. *Journal of Developmental & Behavioral Pediatrics*, *33*(1), 9–16.

Lalli, G. S. (2023). 'In most supermarkets food does not cost £3 per day …' The impact of the school food voucher scheme during COVID-19. *British Educational Research Journal*, *49*(1), 53–69.

Lambie-Mumford, H. (2017). *Hungry Britain: the rise of food charity*. Policy Press.

REFERENCES

Lambie-Mumford, H. (2019). The growth of food banks in Britain and what they mean for social policy. *Critical Social Policy*, *39*(1), 3–22.

Lambie-Mumford, H., & Dowler, E. (2014). Rising use of 'food aid' in the United Kingdom. *British Food Journal*, *116*(9), 1418–25.

Lambie-Mumford, H., & Loopstra, R. (2020). Food banks and the UK welfare state. In H. Lambie-Mumford & T. Silvasti (Eds), *The rise of food charity in Europe* (pp 191–218). Policy Press.

Lambie-Mumford, H., & Silvasti, T. (2020). *The rise of food charity in Europe*. Policy Press.

Lester, D. (2020). Hierarchy of Needs (Maslow). In V. Zeigler-Hill & T. K. Shackelford (Eds), *Encyclopedia of personality and individual differences* (pp 1939–44). Springer International Publishing.

Leung, C. W., Laraia, B. A., Feiner, C., Solis, K., Stewart, A. L., Adler, N. E., et al (2022). The psychological distress of food insecurity: a qualitative study of the emotional experiences of parents and their coping strategies. *Journal of the Academy of Nutrition & Dietetics*, *122*(10), 1903–10.

Lindow, P., Yen, I. H., Xiao, M., & Leung, C. W. (2022). 'You run out of hope': an exploration of low-income parents' experiences with food insecurity using Photovoice. *Public Health Nutrition*, *25*(4), 987–93.

Littler, J. (2017). *Against meritocracy: culture, power and myths of mobility*. Routledge.

Livingstone, N. (2017). Franchising the disenfranchised? The paradoxical spaces of food banks. In A. Ince & S. M. Hall (Eds), *Sharing economies in times of crisis: practices, politics and possibilities* (pp 110–24). Routledge.

Loopstra, R., & Tarasuk, V. (2012). The relationship between food banks and household food insecurity among low-income Toronto families. *Canadian Public Policy*, *38*(4), 497–514.

Loopstra, R., & Tarasuk, V. (2015). Food bank usage is a poor indicator of food insecurity: insights from Canada. *Social Policy & Society*, *14*(3), 443–55.

Lopez, I., De Andraca, I., Perales, C. G., Heresi, E., Castillo, M., & Colombo, M. (1993). Breakfast omission and cognitive performance of normal, wasted and stunted schoolchildren. *European Journal of Clinical Nutrition*, *47*(8), 533–42.

Lucas, M., Classick, R., Skipp, A., & Julius, J. (2023). Cost-of-living crisis: impact on schools. National Foundation for Educational Research. Retrieved 20 September 2024 from https://www.nfer.ac.uk/publications/cost-of-living-crisis-impact-on-schools/

Markowitz, A. J., Johnson, A. D., & Hines, C. T. (2021). Food insecurity in toddlerhood and school readiness: mediating pathways through parental well-being and behaviors. In B. H. Fiese & A. D. Johnson (Eds), *Food insecurity in families with children: integrating research, practice, and policy* (pp 11–32). Springer Nature Switzerland.

Mazzoli Smith, L., & Todd, L. (2019). Conceptualising poverty as a barrier to learning through 'poverty proofing the school day': the genesis and impacts of stigmatisation. *British Educational Research Journal*, 45(2), 356–71.

McLaughlin, K. A., Green, J. G., Alegría, M., Jane Costello, E., Gruber, M. J., Sampson, N. A., et al (2012). Food insecurity and mental disorders in a national sample of US adolescents. *Journal of the American Academy of Child & Adolescent Psychiatry*, 51(12), 1293–303.

Merrick, R. (2017). Chancellor Philip Hammond accused of more 'failed austerity' after demanding extra spending cuts before the election. *The Independent*. Retrieved 29 July 2024 from https://www.independent.co.uk/news/uk/politics/chancellor-philip-hammond-latest-budget-spending-cuts-austerity-social-care-john-mcdonnell-a7603096.html

Mitchell, J. C. (1984). Typicality and the case study. In R. F. Ellen (Ed), *Ethnographic research: a guide to general conduct* (pp 237–41). Academic Press.

Moss, G., Allen, R., Bradbury, A., Duncan, S., Harmey, S., & Levy, R. (2020). Primary teachers' experience of the COVID-19 lockdown: eight key messages for policymakers going forward. UCL Institute of Education. Retrieved 20 September 2024 from https://discovery.ucl.ac.uk/id/eprint/10103669

REFERENCES

Moss, G., Bradbury, A., Braun, A., Duncan, S., & Levy, R. (2021). Learning through disruption: using schools' experiences of Covid to build a more resilient education system. UCL Institute of Education. Retrieved 20 September 2024 from https://discovery.ucl.ac.uk/id/eprint/10136102/

NAHT (2022). NAHT survey shows the majority of schools in England are looking at redundancies due to the funding crisis. Retrieved 22 July 2024 from https://www.naht.org.uk/Our-Priorities/Other-policy-areas/Policy-research/ArtMID/591/ArticleID/1894/NAHT-survey-shows-the-majority-of-schools-in-England-are-looking-at-redundancies-due-to-the-funding-crisis

NEU (2023). State of education: child poverty. National Education Union. Retrieved 20 September 2024 from https://neu.org.uk/press-releases/state-education-child-poverty

O'Connell, R., Knight, A., & Brannen, J. (2019a). Food poverty in context: parental sacrifice and children's experiences in low income families in the UK. In U. Gustafsson, R. O'Connell, A. Draper, & A. Tonner (Eds), *What is food? Researching a topic with many meanings* (pp 32–50). Routledge.

O'Connell, R., Owen, C., Padley, M., Simon, A., & Brannen, J. (2019b). Which types of family are at risk of food poverty in the UK? A relative deprivation approach. *Social Policy & Society*, *18*(1), 1–18.

O'Hara, M. (2015). *Austerity bites: a journey to the sharp end of cuts in the UK*. Policy Press.

Palmer, A. (2011). Nursery schools for the few or the many? Childhood, education and the State in mid-twentieth-century England. *Paedagogica Historica*, *47*(1–2), 139–54.

Parnham, J. C., Laverty, A. A., Majeed, A., & Vamos, E. P. (2020). Half of children entitled to free school meals did not have access to the scheme during COVID-19 lockdown in the UK. *Public Health*, *187*, 161–4.

Patrick, R., Power, M., Garthwaite, K., Kaufman, J., Page, G., & Pybus, K. (2022). *A year like no other: life on a low income during COVID-19*. Policy Press.

Patrick, R., & Pybus, K. (2022). Cost of living crisis: we cannot ignore the human cost of living in poverty. *British Medical Journal*, *377*, o925.

Perryman, J. (2022). *Teacher retention in an age of performative accountability: target culture and the discourse of disappointment*. Routledge.

Perryman, J., Bradbury, A., Calvert, G., & Kilian, K. (2023). Final report of the Beyond Ofsted Inquiry. Beyond Ofsted Inquiry. Retrieved 20 September 2024 from https://beyondofsted.org.uk/reports/

Pourmotabbed, A., Moradi, S., Babaei, A., Ghavami, A., Mohammadi, H., Jalili, C., et al (2020). Food insecurity and mental health: a systematic review and meta-analysis. *Public Health Nutrition*, *23*(10), 1778–90.

Power, M. (2022). *Hunger, whiteness and religion in neoliberal Britain: an inequality of power*. Policy Press.

Power, M., Small, N., Doherty, B., & Pickett, K. E. (2020). The incompatibility of system and lifeworld understandings of food insecurity and the provision of food aid in an English city. *Voluntas: International Journal of Voluntary & Nonprofit Organizations*, *31*(5), 907–22.

Purdam, K., Garratt, E. A., & Esmail, A. (2015). Hungry? Food insecurity, social stigma and embarrassment in the UK. *Sociology*, *50*(6), 1072–88.

Pybus, K., Power, M., & Pickett, K. E. (2021). 'We are constantly overdrawn, despite not spending money on anything other than bills and food': a mixed-methods, participatory study of food and food insecurity in the context of income inequality. *Journal of Poverty & Social Justice*, *29*(1), 21–45.

Quick, L. (2024a). The SATs effect: the verdict from year 6 teachers. More than a Score. Retrieved 21 May 2024 from https://www.morethanascore.org.uk/wp-content/uploads/2024/05/TheSATsEffect.pdf

Quick, L. (2024b). The threat of three-fold failure: 'low attainers' in English primary schools. *British Journal of Sociology of Education*, *45*(4), 369–54.

REFERENCES

Redmond, G., Skattebol, J., Hamilton, M., Andresen, S., & Woodman, R. (2022). Projects-of-self and projects-of-family: young people's responsibilisation for their education and responsibility for care. *British Journal of Sociology of Education*, *43*(1), 84–103.

Riches, G. (2002). Food banks and food security: welfare reform, human rights and social policy. Lessons from Canada? *Social Policy & Administration*, *36*(6), 648–63.

Riches, G. (2020). Foreword. In H. Lambie-Mumford & T. Silvasti (Eds), *The rise of food charity in Europe* (pp xi–xviii). Policy Press.

Ridge, T. (2013). 'We are all in this together'? The hidden costs of poverty, recession and austerity policies on Britain's poorest children. *Children & Society*, *27*(5), 406–17.

Smith, D., & Thompson, C. (2022). *Food deserts and food insecurity in the UK: exploring social inequality*. Routledge.

Sosenko, F., Littlewood, M., Bramley, G., Fitzpatrick, S., Blenkinsopp, J., & Wood, J. (2019). A study of poverty and food insecurity in the UK. The Trussell Trust. Retrieved 28 July 2024 from https://www.stateofhunger.org/wp-content/uploads/2019/11/State-of-Hunger-Report-November2019-Digital.pdf

Strong, S. (2019). The vital politics of foodbanking: hunger, austerity, biopower. *Political Geography*, *75*(3), 102053.

Tarkiainen, L. (2022). *Deservingness in welfare policy and practice: discursive and rhetorical approaches*. Routledge.

Timmins, N. (2021). Universal Credit's £20-a-week increase: a looming headache for the chancellor. Institute for Government. Retrieved 29 July 2024 from https://www.instituteforgovernment.org.uk/article/comment/universal-credits-ps20-week-increase-looming-headache-chancellor

Townsend, P. (1979). *Poverty in the United Kingdom: a survey of household resources and standards of living*. University of California Press.

Treanor, M. C. (2020). *Child poverty: aspiring to survive*. Policy Press.

Try, L. (2024). Catastrophic caps: an analysis of the impact of the two-child limit and the benefit cap. Resolution Foundation. Retrieved 29 July 2024 from https://www.resolutionfoundation.org/publications/catastophic-caps/

UK Government (2024). Schools, pupils and their characteristics. GOV.UK. Retrieved 22 July 2024 from https://explore-education-statistics.service.gov.uk/find-statistics/school-pupils-and-their-characteristics

United Nations World Food Programme (2006). Hunger and learning. Retrieved 20 September 2024 from https://docs.wfp.org/api/documents/WFP-0000118955/download/?_ga=2.90406426.1451247341.1681923175-1267229146.1681923175

Vince, S. (2024). *Disciplinary power in early childhood education and care funding policies in England: how the 15 and 30 hours are exacerbating 'splits'*. University College London.

Vitamin Angels (nd). Vitamin Angels – home. Retrieved 1 August 2024 from https://vitaminangels.org/

Wainwright, E., Hoskins, K., Arabaci, R., Zhai, J., Gao, J., & Xu, Y. (2024). Researching the everyday educational lives of low-income families: the importance of researcher and participant contexts. *British Journal of Educational Studies*, 1–21.

Ward, K. P., & Lee, S. J. (2020). Mothers' and fathers' parenting stress, responsiveness, and child wellbeing among low-income families. *Children & Youth Services Review*, *116*, 105218.

Weinreb, L., Wehler, C., Perloff, J., Scott, R., Hosmer, D., Sagor, L., et al (2002). Hunger: its impact on children's health and mental health. *Pediatrics*, *110*(4), e41.

Wells, R., & Caraher, M. (2014). UK print media coverage of the food bank phenomenon: from food welfare to food charity? *British Food Journal*, *116*(9), 1426–45.

Williams, A., Cloke, P., May, J., & Goodwin, M. (2016). Contested space: the contradictory political dynamics of food banking in the UK. *Environment & Planning A: Economy and Space*, *48*(11), 2291–316.

Wise, J. (2021). Reverse cuts to children's centres, peers urge government. *British Medical Journal*, *375*, n2851.

Wyse, D., Bradbury, A., & Trollope, R. (2022). Assessment for children's learning: The Independent Commission on Assessment in Primary Education (ICAPE) final report. NEU. Retrieved 13 October 2023 from https://www.icape.org.uk/

REFERENCES

Youdell, D., & Lindley, M. R. (2018). *Biosocial education: the social and biological entanglements of learning*. Routledge.

Zaslow, M., Bronte-Tinkew, J., Capps, R., Horowitz, A., Moore, K. A., & Weinstein, D. (2009). Food security during infancy: implications for attachment and mental proficiency in toddlerhood. *Maternal & Child Health Journal, 13*(1), 66–80.

Index

Note: References to tables appear in **bold** type.

A

accountability systems, framework 2, 5, 128, 140–3, 149
ADHD 88
advantages, of food banks in school 100–1
  awareness on family needs 103–5
  confidentiality, in location of food banks 123
  easy to access 117–20
  home–school relationships improvement 101–2
  improved connections and trust 105–10
  moral justifications 113–16
  reducing stigma 120–6
Anderson, S. A. 33
anxiety 31–2, 77, 120
austerity 12, 146, 147
  policies 4, 20, 25, 61
  role in food insecurity 24–6, 39, 62

B

Baker, W. 1–2, 22–3, 53, 61, 150
basic needs, language 23, 68, 73
biosocial education 29–30
Bloody Good Period 58
Booth Primary School **14**, **16**, 42, 43, 48, 50–1, 57, 62, 64, 91, 93, 107–8, 115, 118, 123, 136

Bradbury, A 3, 10, 13, 28, 146
Braun, A. 135, 137
breakfast clubs 1, 22–3, 134
British Education Research Association (BERA) 13, 19
Brown Pre-School **15**, **17**, 45–7, 54, 88, 93, 95, 112, 115, 131
budgets
  in families 86–7
  and food bank operations 137–9
  local authority budgets 24
  in schools 25, 28, 50, 142

C

Caraher, M. 45, 61
Chartwells 27
Chefs in Schools study (2022) 30
child and adolescent mental health unit 129–30
Child Care 25, 136
child poverty 1–2, 9, 23, 94
  and education, relationship between 23–4
  and food banks in school 23, 130–2
  schools responsibilisation 128, 143, 149–51
child protection issues 115–16
child tax credit 25
childminders 7
children's centres 7–9

INDEX

children's learning impacts 14, 16, 80, 97
  behavioural issues 76–7
  brain development 73
  concentration 71–3
  on free breakfast provision 74
City Harvest 42
civil society 11–12
Cloke, P. 36, 38, 147–8
cognitive function, impact of inadequate food on 30–1, 72
community shop 61
community-embedded schools 142
Conservative and Liberal Democrat Coalition government 24
cost-of-living crisis 1, 3–5, 28–9
  and Covid pandemic 63–4
  educational responses to 129
  and food donations 48–9
Covid pandemic 3, 14, 40–1, 61, 65, 67–8, 125
  as crisis policy enactment 10, 28, 134
  and education context 5–6
  and food banks development 62–4
  impacts of 26–8
  post-Covid recovery plan 75
  pre-Covid era 145–6
crisis policy enactment 10, 28, 40–1, 68, 134, 145–6
culturally appropriate food 44

D

deficit discourses about families 71, 98, 112, 134
  budgeting issues 86–7
  control and discipline, lack of 91–2
  dependency problem 112–13
  deservingness 94
  food choices 88–92, 145
  housing issues 8, 34, 95–7, 130
  local food environment, problems of 89–90
  parenting and behaviour practices 71, 88–9, 92–3
  sympathetic comments 87–8
  taking advantage 93–4, 98, 110

Department for Education 10
depression and stress in parents 31–2
deserving and undeserving poor trope 34–5, 38, 71, 93, 94, 98
deservingness 33, 34–5, 94, 97, 145
diet
  balanced adequate diet 30–1
  and behaviour 89
  and hyperactivity 88
  see also nutritious food
Dimbleby Nursery **15**, **17**, 47, 49, 54, 64, 94, 95, 104, 114, 118–19, 122–3, 138
disparities between schools 128, 140–3, 149–50
distributing food, by schools 42, 45, 61, 62, 68
  choice provision and limitations in 53–6
  families needing support, identifying 49–53
  food pantry/club 56–7
domestic violence 86, 115–16
donations 19, 38, 59
  cost-of-living crisis reduces 48–9
  from food redistribution organisations 41–2, 44, 62, 124
  of non-food goods 58–9, 104
  sourcing food by 45–8

E

Early Years Foundation Stage (EYFS) 6, 7
Early Years Settings, Food Banks in
  analysis of datasets 18–19
  case study settings 13–15, **14**
  ethical issues 19–20
  interview with participants 15–18, **17**
edible waste 32, 45
  see also food waste
education and welfare, tensions between 114–15
educational attainment 23–4
emergency food aid 32, 61

emergent parallel charity economy 12
ethnographic work in food banks 38, 87
eugenicist ideas 29
'extras' provision, in food bank 82–3

F

family stress 22, 39, 84
 and financial insecurity 78
 and hunger 31–2
FareShare 32, 42
faulty behavioural practices 38
Felix Project 18, 32, 42, 45, 61, 62, 124, 131
Field Nursery School **15**, **17**, 42, 45, 62, 97, 105, 125
financial insecurity and family stress 78
fitting in, emotional impact of 80–2
food aid 12, 23, 37–8, 53
food charities 11, 37–8, 46, 61, 150
 in education 2, 23
 problem with 49
 and responsibilisation 144
food club *see* food pantry
food insecurity 2–3, 9, 22, 26, 60, 65–6
 and domestic violence 86
 and family stress 31–2, 78–9
 and learning impacts 30–1
 and poverty 34
 and reduced physical activity 73–4
 social acceptability 33
 stigmatising families 33–4
food pantry 15–16, 32, 58, 60, 123
 culturally appropriate food, provision of 44–5
 limitations of 50
 location and easy access of 118
 operation of 41, 56–7, 120, 123–4
 for sanctuary seekers 96–7
 volunteers in 139–40

see also community shop; food stall
food redistribution organisations 41–3, 45, 49, 60–1
food security at home 77–8
food stall 122
food waste 2, 20, 42, 59–61, 122, 125
see also edible waste
Foucauldian analysis of biopower 37
Foucault, M. 9–10, 143–4
free school meals (FSM) 1, 24, 142–3
free uniform provision 80–2
funding 8, 23, 49, 55, 111–12, 128, 149–50
 and cost-of-living crisis 28–9
 crisis 7
 cuts and challenges 25–6
 fundraising activities 139–40
 Pupil Premium funding 24, 142–3
 school staff funding 47–8
see also donations
Furey, S. 45, 61

G

Garthwaite, K. 38, 57, 87, 109, 112
global financial crash (2008) 24
Good Samaritan narrative 37–8
governmentality literature 36–7, 143–5
green agenda 41, 59–61, 68

H

Health in Pregnancy Grant 25
Helen Hamlyn Centre for Pedagogy 13
Hierarchy of Needs (Maslow) 73
home learning 5
home–school relationships 101–2
human right to food 36
hunger 29, 36, 37, 59, 70, 113–14, 148, 149
 depoliticisation of 38, 61, 144, 147

INDEX

effects on learning 30–1
on family stress 31–2
impacts on concentration and brain development 71–4, 97–8
and responsibilisation of schools 2–4, 10, 11–12
Hygiene Project 57

I

impacts, of school-based food banks 70–1
on children's learning 71–4
on children's wellbeing 77–80
deficit discourses about families 86–94
on family wellbeing 84–6
on particular groups of families 95–7
physical impacts and behaviour of children 74–7
social impacts 80–4
inadequate food intake 30–1
individual responsibility 11–13, 37, 144–5, 148
Institute for Fiscal Studies 7
Institute of Education (IOE) 3, 19
interactions, importance of 32, 108

J

Johnson, B. 62
Jones, B. M. A. 146

K

key person 'expert' in local families 103–5
Konzelmann, S. J. 24

L

Lambie-Mumford, H. 38–9, 49
Lansbury Primary School 42, 50, 95–6, 110, 142
learning loss 4
Lindley, M. R. 29
local food providers 46–7
low-income families 23–4, 64

M

maintained nursery school (MNS) 7–8, 14–15, **15**, 25–6
malnutrition 75
Monday Charitable Trust 13
mood disorders 31–2
moral obligation of schools 28, 113–16, 126, 135–7
Moss, G. 27–8
multi-academy trusts (MATs) 6–7

N

National Association of Headteachers 7
National Curriculum 6
National Education Union 30
National Health Service (NHS) 8, 147
Neighbourly app 45
neoliberal governmentality 36–7
neoliberal processes of individualisation 2, 10–12, 35, 38, 86–7, 129, 143, 146–8
neuroscience in education 29, 73
NGOs 47
non-food goods provision 1, 57–9
non-perishable goods 58
nutritious food 44, 47, 92

O

O'Connell, R. 30
Ofsted 5, 6, 65–6, 140–2
Oliver Children's Centre 15–16, **17**, 41, 42, 44, 49, 50, 56, 57, 64, 96, 105, 120, 123, 139–40
operation, of school-based food banks 41
  distributing food 49–57
  donations and funding 48–9
  non-food provision 57–9
  sourcing food 41–8
origin and development, of food banks in schools
  austerity policy impacts 61–2
  cost-of-living crisis impacts 64–8
  Covid pandemic impacts 62–4
  to support school staffs 67–7

P

parent–child interactions, negative 32
Peabody Primary School **14**, **16**, 47, 53, 59, 79, 80–1, 83, 116, 124
physical impacts and behaviour of children 74–7
Pickett, K. E. 12
piecemeal provision 62
policy enactment 10, 40, 68
  budgetary issues 137–9
  fundraising activities 139–40
  moral obligations of schools 135–7
  and policy vacuum on food insecurity 134–5
  see also crisis policy enactment
policy sociology 9–10, 128–9
policy vacuum 134–40
poor nutrition impacts on children 75, 90, 94
post-pandemic hopes (Bradbury) 5, 146
Power, M. 33, 37
practical justification, of food provision 117
  easy to access food banks 117–20
  stigma and shame, reducing 120–6
primary education 6–7
Primary Schools, Food Banks in 13
  analysis of datasets 18–19
  austerity, role of 24–6
  biosocial perspectives 29–30
  case study schools 13–15, **15**
  cost-of-living crisis 28–9
  Covid pandemic impacts 26–8
  ethical issues 19–20
  hunger and family stress impacts on learning 30–2
  interview with participants 15–18, **16**
  neoliberal solutions to poverty 32–9
  poverty and education, relationship between 23–4
  and social interactions 33–4

private, voluntary and independent (PVI) providers 7–8
public awareness, about food banks 125
public food banks 2, 3, 86–7, 102, 109, 117
  vs school food banks 32, 102, 118–20, 126, 149
  and withdrawal of state 129, 146, 147
public spending cuts 24
Pupil Premium funding 24, 142–3
Purdham, K. 34
Pybus, K. 33

R

Rashford, M. 26–7
Rashford Nursery School 7, **15**, **17**, 41, 48, 52–3, 74, 82, 88, 93, 95, 119, 131, 137
Reception classes 7, 23–4
recognition of food banks, lack of 141–3
relationships
  difficulties in 110–13
  improved connections and trust 105–10
  interactions for building 51–2, 108–9
  school-parent relationships 18, 86, 101–2, 105–6, 111, 123, 149
  staff and parents relationship 53, 54
responsibilisation 9, 21
  addressing hunger 2, 11–12
  and power 11–13
  of schools 23, 37, 69, 128, 143–8
retrenchment of public services 26, 129, 148
Riches, G. 12, 45, 148
Rowntree Primary School 7, **14**, **16**, 41, 42, 50, 53, 65–8, 81, 82, 106, 122, 124–5, 140–2
Russia's invasion of Ukraine 5, 28

S

sanctuary seekers 96–7
SAT tests 6, 140–1

INDEX

school newsletters 50–1
school staff funding 47–8
Schools Week article 4
self-harming children 129–30
semi-structured interviews 17
social acceptability 33
social impacts, of food banks in schools 80–4
social interactions and food 33–4
social media, role in food distribution 50
social policy scholarship 12, 143
societal 'regimes of truth' 86–7
sourcing food
  cultural appropriateness of food 44–5
  food donations 46–8
  from food redistribution organisations 41–3, 45, 49, 60–1
  nature of foods received 43–4
  Neighbourly app 45
state-funded schools 7
stay and play groups 7–8
stigmatising families, to use food bank 53–7, 120–5
Strong, S. 34, 37, 49
stunted growth 30–1
Sure Start Centres 25, 26
Sure Start Maternity Grant 25
Sure Start programme (2000) 8
surplus food 32, 33, 41–2, 43, 45, 47, 61, 65

T

taking advantage families 93–4, 98, 110
Tarkiainen, L. 35, 93, 94
teaching union surveys 72
third-sector organisations 11–12
Townsend, P. 80
Trollope, B. 13
Trussell Trust 24, 32, 132–3
Twining Primary School 42, 51, 55, 62, 64–5, 88, 93–4, 103, 106–7, 109, 114, 123, 129–30, 142
two-child benefit cap 25

U

UCL Institute of Education ethical review system 19
UN Universal Declaration of Human Rights 36
underserved communities 46–7
underweight children 76
undeservingness 35, 93
Universal Credit 25, 27, 28, 65
universal human point of connection 107

V

Vince, S 4, 13
Vitamin Angels 46–7
volunteers, in food banks 12, 34, 37–9, 42, 43, 87, 139–40
vouchers 26–7, 32, 48, 53, 65, 147

W

Webb Primary School **14**, **16**, 43, 45, 47–8, 65, 86, 92, 96, 119, 125
welfare state, withdrawal of 22, 36–7, 39, 129, 146, 147
wellbeing
  of children 77–82, 98, 109, 115
  of families 84–6, 98
wider policy contextual issues 128–34
  cost-of-living crisis 131–3
  retrenchment of public services 129–31
  stagnant wages and benefits 133–4
Williams, A. 38–9
Wilson Nursery School **15**, **17**, 47, 48, 54, 58, 67–8, 74, 108, 120–1, 123
Working Tax Credit 25

Y

Youdell, D. 29